TOWN ORIGINS

The Evidence from Medieval England

TOWN ORIGINS

The Evidence from Medieval England

Edited with an introduction by

John F. Benton

CALIFORNIA INSTITUTE OF TECHNOLOGY

D. C. HEATH AND COMPANY
Lexington, Massachusetts

To the memory of Robert L. Reynolds

Printed in the United States of America

Library of Congress Number: 67-25412

Table of Contents

List of Maps

Introduction

THE GROWING SIZE, wealth and power of cities continue to transform the modern world. We are familiar today with an industrial economy, political centralization and secularism. When we take a long view of history we see in the middle ages an agrarian economy, feudalism and institutional religion shaping the lives and thoughts of men. How can we explain these changes? Of great importance, perhaps the most significant single factor, is the growth of towns and all that goes with it, including urban commerce and manufacture and the social and intellectual modes and political organization of city people. An investigation of how and why towns developed in medieval Europe is therefore an attempt to understand the roots of our society.

While historians agree on the importance of the subject, they are far from accord on the answers to significant questions about town origins. This volume brings together some of the explanations they have given and a sample of the evidence which will permit the reader to begin to evaluate these answers for himself.

To name and discuss all the historians who have contributed theories about what gave the original impetus to the growth of towns would introduce a confusing mass of detail. Instead, eight major theories are labeled and summarized below, with the warning that a label and a few sentences can seldom express the nuances and complexity of the historian's approach.

Mercantile settlement theory. Towns grew when merchants, involved in long distance commerce, began to settle at attractive locations. These merchants came from outside the ranks of the clergy and the nobility.

Market theory. The economic emphasis here is on local rather than long-distance trade. The special status of the town came from the right to hold a market and protection given to it.

Artisanal theory. The division of labor between agriculture and handicrafts created a settled class of town-dwellers. The emphasis here is not on trade but production.

Association or gild theory. Private associations, formed perhaps for social or religious purposes, acquired economic and political power. Their united strength won them special liberties.

Military theory. Towns were first established as defensive centers. The garrison, perhaps the men of different lords, required a special court and special law, the king's peace.

Ecclesiastical theory. A great church, either monastic or episcopal, attracted a settled population. Immunities and privileges granted to the church gave a special status to the settlement around it. This theory of course implies that churchmen took a shrewd interest in the commercial success of their town.

Free village theory. The liberties of the town developed directly from those of the village. This theory assumes the existence of villages with a significant amount of self-government.

Romanist theory. Medieval towns were a direct continuation of ancient, Roman towns. Like the previous theory, this explanation places its emphasis on continuity rather than change.

Not all these theories are exclusive, but even when compatible ones are combined, questions of priority or emphasis are important. Did a military garrison, merchants, or artisans come first, and which was most significant in establishing the character of the town? Did townsmen win their liberties or were they attracted by them?

By now the reader may well have noted the close relationship of the question "What makes a town?" to "What is a town?" If a town is defined as a place with an economy markedly different from that of the countryside, then economic changes, either in commerce or production, must have played a significant role in its origin. If it is a place with a special legal status, then its origins can be associated with the acquisition of its liberties. If it is simply a concentration of people, then only the proponents of the free village theory are untroubled by the problem of distinguishing between a large village and a small town. If it is defined in physical terms, the construction of a wall is usually the most significant factor in distinguishing a medieval town.

The close relationship of a theory of origins with what one considers characteristic of a town had its effect on the development of the historical controversy being considered. In general terms, the two major categories of theories are legal and economic. Historians of the nineteenth century, deeply involved with questions of constitutional development, tended to place their primary emphasis on the origin of urban liberties. In contrast, when Henri Pirenne (1862–1935) first published his mercantile settlement theory in 1893, he heralded the new direction of historical involvement with economic explanations.

Pirenne, one of the most productive and incisive of twentieth-century historians, continued to refine and establish his theory; the selection which introduces this collection was published in 1933, two years before his death. It is an appropriate introduction to current thought, for Pirenne's thesis became the most influential explanation of town origins in the first half of this century.[1]

Partly this success was the result of the cogency of his arguments and evidence; partly it resulted from the contemporary predisposition to accept economic explanations. But it was also due to Pirenne's amazing ability as a scholar to perceive patterns and relationships, and his skill as a writer in presenting these insights clearly and effectively to a popular audience. Pirenne has had his scholarly critics, but none has attacked his thesis in terms as simple and effective as his own.

For a direct rebuttal of Pirenne's thesis we turn to an author who calls himself "a generalist, not a specialist in any field." In his *The City in History* Lewis Mumford (1895–) covers the sweep of civilization from ancient Mesopotamia to the present. His work is based on vast reading in secondary works, rather than the primary sources of the specialist. His perspective leads him to counter the fundamental tenets of Pirenne's position, while reasserting a combination of several older theories. His challenge to the mercantile settlement theory is as simple and forceful as Pirenne's original statement.

Mr. Mumford's explanation, as one would expect in a work of such scope, draws attention to a few basic patterns. The next selection places its primary emphasis on the complexity of medieval urban development. Edith Ennen avoids an attempt to find an explanation for the origin of *the* medieval European town. There were many towns, and diverse factors influenced their origin and growth. But for Professor Ennen complexity does not imply random development. Calling attention to different regions and different types of towns, she distinguishes a number of superimposed patterns which reveal a certain order underlying the diversity of urban forms.

[1] This mercantile settlement thesis is closely related to his explanation of the transition from the ancient to the medieval world, presented by Alfred Havighurst as *The Pirenne Thesis* in this series.

Her historical typology, with its emphasis on variety, may suggest to the reader that he is in no position to evaluate any theory of medieval urban origins until he has studied the history of towns in all the regions of Europe. In deference to this reaction, which has some justification, we turn now to a case study of England to permit concentration on a limited and clearly defined region. The theories popular on the continent have in one way or another been applied to England too. And thanks to the comparative wealth of surviving English evidence, the reader will be able to test these theories against medieval sources.

William Stubbs (1825–1901), Regius Professor of Modern History at Oxford and later bishop of that city, and Frederic William Maitland (1850–1906), Downing Professor of the Laws of England at Cambridge, were the two most influential English medieval historians of the nineteenth century. Both explained the legal and constitutional development of English towns with reference to contemporary German scholarship. Although he noted the economic importance of trade, Stubbs explained the legal origins of the borough by applying to England the free village community theory then popular on the continent. Maitland first published his military or "garrison" theory in a review of a book on the constitutional origins of German towns.

Our selection on the particular case of England begins, however, not with the work of these masters, nor with other writing from the end of the nineteenth century when English historians were focusing on the early history of their towns, but with a criticism of current theories written at the turn of the century by a French scholar, Charles Petit-Dutaillis (1868–1947). Using the perspective provided by thorough knowledge of French institutions, Petit-Dutaillis reviewed the Romanist theory, which then had some popularity in England, the work of Stubbs and Maitland, and the contributions of Mary Bateson (1865–1906), a Cambridge scholar who, after collaborating with Maitland, became one of England's most indefatigable workers on municipal records. Carefully avoiding a unitary approach, Petit-Dutaillis emphasized that different causes could favor the growth of towns, and he judiciously picked from the writing of his predecessors the explanations he found most acceptable.

Little new work was contributed in the next generation, except for the book *Burgage Tenure in England,* published in 1914 by an American, Morley deWolf Hemmeon. His investigation of burgage tenure, that is, holding — in return for fixed money rent — town property which could be sold or conveyed by inheritance, led him to see this privilege as the peculiar mark of a borough. This view, like Miss Bateson's that the special characteristic of a borough was a borough court, was another refinement of the study of the borough through its definition in legal terms.

The entire legal and constitutional approach was challenged by another American, Carl Stephenson (1886–1954), who had studied under Pirenne in 1924–25. In 1926 he published his first article on the origin of English towns, and in 1933 he developed these ideas, with some modifications, in a book entitled *Borough and Town.* This title sets forth his thesis in brief. The Anglo-Saxon boroughs were simply military and administrative establishments; they were not towns, for he saw the essential characteristic of a town as commerce, which in his opinion did not develop on a large scale in England until about the time of the Norman Conquest. Reducing his final view to a sentence, he submitted that "the history of the English borough can best be understood by regarding the medieval town as essentially a mercantile settlement." Eventually the terms "borough" and "town" became equivalent, he wrote, but they should not be treated as such in the Anglo-Saxon period.

Stephenson's book was answered three years later by James Tait (1863–1944), the leading English authority on medieval urban history. In *The Medieval English Borough,* whose title proclaims a counter-attack, Tait refuted Stephenson on point after point of detail so effectively that in following years many English medievalists simply omitted the American author from their bibliographies and consideration. When an English scholar, referring to the problem of the Old English borough, wrote in 1962 that "the best mode of entry into any discussion of the matter lies through the scholarly differences of opinion in the early 1930's between Professors Carl Stephenson and James Tait," he was according Stephenson a posthumous rehabilitation.

But students who attempt to settle this problem for themselves by reading the two authors together often find that their understanding is not advanced. Like Pirenne, Stephenson wrote clearly and effectively, and it is easy to see what he is saying. Tait's book, the work of his declining years, is learned but far from lucid. Though some judged him to have won on points, Tait did not knock out his opponent with a clear explanation of his own.

If economic matters alone are considered, the selections presented here may, in fact, lead the reader to wonder what the fuss was about. There seems to be only a difference of emphasis or timing, with Stephenson saying there was less commerce before the conquest than some have said, and Tait replying that there was more than Stephenson recognized. Both readily agreed that England was not nearly so economically developed before the conquest as it later became.

But when Tait concluded of the English borough that "its humble origins should not be ignored," he seemed to have more in mind than embryonic commerce. In Stephenson's view long-distance trade, and that alone, made the medieval English town. He challenges the reader to weigh the importance for the origin of the English town of all other factors against that of European commerce. Tait's reply raises the question of the degree to which the location, institutions, importance and character of English towns were already established before the great revival of European commerce of the late eleventh century. And one may also ask how many, if any, medieval English towns were never significantly affected by long-distance trade.

The collection of controversial writing is concluded by a review which presents the thesis of a Russian scholar, Yakov Levitsky. The theory that the population which created towns was composed of artisans and craftsmen is the orthodox doctrine of Marxist historical thought. As a result of a growing division of labor, towns became markets for agricultural production, and townsmen produced manufactured goods, such as iron ploughshares, required by country people. According to this theory, which Professor Levitsky elaborated about England in 1960, no middlemen at all were necessary for the development of towns.

In any historical controversy final judgments can not be made on the basis of the author's reputation, the plausibility of his views, or the grace of his style, but only by evaluation of the evidence. In the second half of the book the reader is provided with a sample of the major sources available to any historian who wishes to investigate the origin of English towns. Although most of the original footnote citations have been omitted from the secondary works included here, wherever possible references to the sources which follow have been substituted.

The initial problem for which these sources can be used is that of defining a borough or town without immediately introducing a subjective evaluation. Medieval people could be maddeningly imprecise in their terminology, and the line between a borough and a market town or village was not sharply drawn in the middle ages. The safest approach is to avoid simple labels and see what places at any given time were treated as different from the countryside. Tenth-century laws tell us that no coins were to be minted except in a town, that all purchases above a certain value should take place in a town, that borough defenses were to be repaired once a year, and that the borough court should be held three times a year.[2] When we find an Anglo-Saxon locality with a wall, a mint, a legally acceptable market and a court, we may consider that it was significantly different from the ordinary village.

Unfortunately only two of these four characteristics can be established for a satisfactory number of places. We have no list of borough courts. Markets were included unsystematically in the eleventh-century Domesday Book, but the list is nowhere near inclusive and places with no other claim to consideration were said to have markets.[3] Archaeology and written records do combine, however, to tell us of many Anglo-Saxon military centers. And since the mints have left us tangible evidence of their production, we can usually establish their location. In short, we can map defensive centers and mints, and that is a start.

This beginning can be continued by listing all the places in Domesday Book called boroughs or said to have a burgess population, and this information can often be supplemented by a rough estimate of population. In the twelfth century we have an indication of special standing through the payment of a special borough tax and the existence of town charters. And finally, we have a form of population census in the poll tax records of the late fourteenth century.

The maps, so designed that when precisely superimposed a pin stuck into a spot on one can pierce the same location on a map below, have a special value for showing what Professor Ennen calls "the shift of the town's center of gravity." In the early thirteenth century New Sarum or Salisbury was established less than two miles from Old Sarum, which was left to rot, and in the same way (Old) Windsor shifted to New Windsor. Here the names reveal the change, but only location shows the virtual identity of Domesday Tanshelf and later Pontefract. And there was apparently some sort of continuity when Totnes and Barnstable in Devonshire replaced Halwell and Pilton.

A comparison of these lists and maps, along with that of Roman towns, reveals decay, continuity, and growth. If done mechanically, such comparison shows only the obvious conclusion that some seed fell on rocky ground and the seeds withered away, while other seeds fell upon good soil. But more careful attention will often show what particular conditions were favorable for urban growth or why a given town failed to develop. Some of the materials permit the towns to be ranked in a rough order of size or wealth or precedence, so that the demise of a marginal town which had never taken firm root, like so many of the places which had a population in Domesday Book of a few hundred, need not be equated with that of one like Thetford, which was once important. A special concentration of material permits the reader to follow the growth of a few individual towns, including Bath, Bristol, Bury St. Edmunds and London.

Not everyone will wish to undertake a labor which entails some tedium, but detailed comparison can establish a division into urban types and regions which shows, as Professor Ennen did for all of Europe, some of the patterns of the limited area of England. If no unitary explanation proves acceptable, perhaps some factors predominated in certain regions or at certain times. Which boroughs were particularly likely to fail? How many of the leading fourteenth-century towns began in one period or another, and why? How many of them owed their prosperity, directly or indirectly, to European commerce?

While the comparative study of many towns can suggest generalizations, the historian establishes his work on the evidence

[2] Below p. 54.
[3] See Domesday Book on St. Germans, below p. 74.

of particular places, people or institutions. An unusual document shows the precise relationship between the town government and the merchant gild at Ipswich in 1200. We have a description of the goods seized by the men of the abbot of Bury St. Edmunds when they destroyed a neighboring market in 1201. The record survives of the length of time it took to settle a court case at St. Ives in 1270. Part of the pleasure of history consists in working back and forth between generalization and explanation on the one hand and precise and unique evidence on the other.

Historical perspective gives us the advantage of seeing forces at work of which the people affected were not always aware. The conscious attitudes and aspirations of a mass of people also have an effect upon history, but little of their record from the middle ages has survived the ravages of time. Only one Anglo-Saxon poet has told us of his feelings on seeing the ruins of a walled town, and gild regulations tell us but little of the fraternal bond uniting a group of drinking companions. Since the record is scanty, a determined effort must be made to include the human element in our early history.

Research in medieval history has its special problems. The scarcity of evidence means that what exists must be thoroughly squeezed. The distinctions between surely established conclusions and less secure assumptions must be kept clear. Arguments from negative evidence must be treated with suspicion; we may not hear of a borough from royal records because it was in the hands of a baron, or simply because a fragment of parchment was gnawed by rats. The temptation to be more systematic than the evidence permits must be resisted. These counsels do not advise despair, but humility. The study of medieval evidence shows why good scholars can disagree even about simple factual matters.

It would be a sterile exercise if the reader should study these sources only to determine which, if any, of a group of scholars or theories is "right." Historians may, of course, be wrong, and if they are, their theories should be discarded; no view need be accepted simply because it is that of an expert. Still, the positive value of studying an historical controversy is to see what contribution each author has made to the understanding of the complexity of human experience. When the reader tests theory against evidence, he is on the way to being his own historian.

GLOSSARY

BURH, BURG, BOURG Old English, German and French words for a fortified place. *Burh* is the ancestor of "borough."

CASTRUM Latin for a fortified place, a fort or military camp.

CIVITAS, CIVITATES Classical Latin for a city or city-state. In the middle ages it sometimes meant a bishop's see, sometimes any important town.

CNIHT Old English term for a servant or retainer. Since such men were often armed and mounted, the word developed into "knight," but originally it had no chivalric significance. Etymologically *cnihtengild* meant an association of retainers. Perhaps the independent merchants of the *cnihtengild* of London were descendants of stewards placed by their masters in the town.

EARL'S THIRD PENNY When an Earl received as his due one third of the revenues of a court, his income was given this name.

GAFOL Old English for "tax" or "tribute." Like *landgabel* it came to mean a property rent.

HAW A place enclosed by a fence or hedge, often a town property.

MISKENNING Verbal error in reciting a formal oath or in pleading before a court, causing one to lose his suit.

SAC AND SOC An alliterative phrase which sometimes meant vaguely "justice and jurisdiction." When used more precisely, *soc* meant the right to hold a "private" court.

THEGN Like *cniht,* originally a servant. But since to be the retainer of a great man could be a highly honorable status, *thegn* came to mean a man who ranked above a *ceorl,* the ordinary freeman.

VILLA In medieval Latin the word meant either a town or a rural center, a township.

VILLE NEUVE French term for a newly established town, often one with attractive liberties.

The Conflict of Opinion

"The primitive bourgeoisie was exclusively composed of men living by trade. The reason why they came, before the end of the eleventh century, to be known by the word *bourgeois,* which was really much better suited to the inhabitants of the old burgs, at the foot of which they settled, is to be found in the fact that very early the mercantile group too surrounded itself by a wall or palisade for the sake of security and thus became a burg in its turn."

—HENRI PIRENNE

"The revival of trade is often taken, even by excellent scholars like Pirenne, as the direct cause of the city building and civilizing activities that took place in the eleventh century. But before this could happen a surplus of rural products and a surplus of population were necessary, to provide both goods for trade and customers to purchase them. If the merchants themselves had been the chief occupants of the new cities, they would have had to take in each other's washing."

— LEWIS MUMFORD

"Yet if we go back to the early years of the tenth century, we shall still find this contrast between the borough and the mere township existing as a contrast whence legal consequences flow. Where lies the contrast? What is it that makes a borough to be a borough? That is the problem that we desire to solve. It is a legal problem. We are not to ask why some places are thickly populated or why trade has flowed in this or that channel. We are to ask why certain vills are severed from other vills and are called boroughs."

— F. W. MAITLAND

"The rural, agricultural character of the town is particularly remarkable in England during the whole of the Middle Ages. Those who study its history, 'have fields and pastures on their hands.' "

— CHARLES PETIT-DUTAILLIS

"In the feudal ocean which once rolled over northern and western Europe appeared many islands, relics of a submerged and ante-feudal continent. These islands, some of which were artificial and imitative, were the urban communities. The waves of feudalism might wash their walls; in towns of artificial foundation the spray might be flung into the narrow streets, but there their course was stayed. For the borough, *Stadt,* or *ville* had a tenure of its own, the *tenure en bourgage* of Normandy, the *Weichbild* of Germany, the Burgage Tenure of England."

— MORLEY DEW. HEMMEON

"Where the town grew had perhaps stood an ancient royal fortress, perhaps not. Its site may have been a simple village, a cross-roads market, a fishermen's haven, or a cow-pasture. But neither wall nor court, neither king's peace nor toll-gate, neither kine nor herring, possessed the infallible charm of attracting an urban population. For that a more potent magic was required — European commerce."

— Carl Stephenson

"A study of its various phases certainly discourages the old quest of a neat legal definition of the borough, applicable at all periods. Government officials in the fourteenth century found this no easier than does the student of the Burghal Hidage and Domesday Book. Yet, if, with Dr. Stephenson, it is preferred to find the common thread in the gradual development of a trading community, why should its humble beginnings be ignored?"

— James Tait

"Marx and Engels were the first to discover the basic laws of the development of the city. . . . In western Europe a qualitative change occurred in the development of cities in the tenth to twelfth centuries when, in connection with the growth of productive forces and increased social differentiation of labor, a vigorous process of separation of handicrafts from agriculture began, and consequently artisans and merchants were distinguished from the mass of the village population and became concentrated in certain localities."

— Soviet Historical Encyclopedia (1963)

I. GENERAL THEORIES

Commerce Creates Towns

HENRI PIRENNE

No medieval historian of the first half of the twentieth century has been so widely read, so influential, and the subject of so much debate as Henri Pirenne (1862–1935). After his studies at the first historical seminar at the University of Liége, and in Berlin, Leipzig and Paris, Pirenne became a professor at the University of Ghent at the age of 23. His writings in some thirty books and 275 articles covered a vast range, from critical editions of texts and articles on points of detail to a seven-volume history of his native Belgium and books and lectures addressed to a wide popular audience. His *History of Europe from the Invasions to the XVIth Century* was composed while he was a prisoner in Germany during World War I (at which time he also learned Russian), and has the sweeping simplicity of a work written from a learned and disciplined memory. Pirenne's great influence was due in part to his inclination to stress simplicity and to advance hypotheses to explain major historical phenomena. Among his "theses" were explanations of the transition from the ancient to the medieval world, of the stages of what he called the social history of capitalism, and of the development of medieval towns. The following extract, written at the age of 71, summarizes his views on a subject he had been investigating for most of his life. His synthetic work led one of his colleagues to say of him, "He is an architect, not a carpenter." But it must also be said that his great constructions have been methodically criticized by other scholars, and on his major theses historians are still debating whether Pirenne was more right than wrong.

1. THE REVIVAL OF URBAN LIFE

As long as Mediterranean commerce continued to draw Western Europe into its orbit, urban life went on in Gaul as well as in Italy, Spain and Africa. But when the Islamic invasion had bottled up the ports of the Tyrrhenian Sea after bringing the coasts of Africa and Spain under its control, municipal activity rapidly died out. Save in southern Italy and in Venice, where it was maintained thanks to Byzantine trade, it disappeared everywhere. The towns continued in existence, but they lost their population of artisans and merchants and with it all that had survived of the municipal organisation of the Roman Empire.

The "cities," in each of which there resided a bishop, now became no more than centres of the ecclesiastical administration of their dioceses. Thus they preserved considerable importance, no doubt, from the religious point of view, but from the economic point of view none. At most, a small local market, supplied by the peasants round about, provided for the daily needs of the numerous clergy of the cathedral and of the churches or monasteries grouped around it and those of the serfs employed

From *Economic and Social History of Medieval Europe* by Henri Pirenne, pp. 40–57. Reprinted by permission of Harcourt, Brace & World, Inc. and Routledge & Kegan Paul Ltd.

in their service. At the big annual festivals the diocesan population and pilgrims flocking into the city kept up a certain activity, but in none of this are any signs of a revival visible. In reality these episcopal cities were merely living on the country. The bishops and abbots within their walls lived on the rents and dues which they obtained from their estates, and their existence thus rested essentially on agriculture. The cities were the centres not only of religious but also of manorial administration.

In time of war their old walls furnished a refuge to the surrounding population. But during the period of insecurity which set in with the dissolution of the Carolingian Empire, the need for protection became the first necessity of a people threatened in the South by the Saracen incursions and in the North and West by those of the Normans, to which were added, at the beginning of the tenth century, the terrible cavalry raids of the Hungarians. These invasions led on all sides to the construction of new places of refuge. In this period Western Europe became covered with fortified castles, erected by the feudal princes to serve as a shelter for their men. These castles, or, to use the term by which they were customarily designated, these *bourgs* or *burgs,* were usually composed of a rampart of earth or stones, surrounded by a moat and pierced with gates. The villeins from round about were requisitioned to construct and maintain them. A garrison of knights resided inside; a donjon served as the lord's dwelling-place; a church of canons looked after the needs of religion; and barns and granaries were set up to receive the grain, smoked meats and dues of all kinds levied on the manorial peasants, which served to feed the garrison and the people who, in times of peril, came huddling into the fortress with their cattle. Thus the lay burg, like the ecclesiastical city, lived on the land. Neither had any real economic life of its own. They were perfectly compatible with an agricultural civilisation, for, far from opposing it, they may be said to have served in its defence.

But the revival of commerce soon completely altered their character. The first symptoms of its action are observable in the course of the second half of the tenth century. The wandering life of the merchants, the risks of every sort to which they were exposed, in an age when pillage formed one of the means of existence of the smaller nobility, caused them from the very beginning to seek the protection of the walled towns and burgs, which stood at intervals along the rivers or natural routes by which they travelled. During the summer these served as halting-places, during the bad season as wintering-places. The most favourably situated, whether at the foot of an estuary or in a creek, at the confluence of two rivers, or at a spot where the river ceased to be navigable and cargoes had to be unloaded before they could proceed farther, thus became places of passage and of sojourn for merchants and merchandise.

Soon the space that cities and burgs had to offer these new-comers, who became more and more numerous and embarrassing in proportion as trade increased, was no longer sufficient. They were driven to settle outside the walls and to build beside the old burg a new burg, or, to use the term which exactly describes it, a *faubourg* (*forisburgus*), i.e., an outside burg. Thus, close to ecclesiastical towns or feudal fortresses there sprang up mercantile agglomerations, whose denizens devoted themselves to a kind of life which was in complete contrast to that led by the people of the inside town. The word *portus,* often applied in documents of the tenth and eleventh centuries to these settlements, exactly describes their nature. It did not, in fact, signify a port in the modern sense, but a place through which merchandise was carried, and thus a particularly active place of transit. It was from it that in England and in Flanders the inhabitants of the *port* themselves received the name of *poorters* or *portmen,* which was long synonymous with *bourgeois* or *burgess* and indeed described them rather better than the latter, for the primitive bourgeoisie was exclusively composed of men living by trade. The reason why they came, before the end of the eleventh century, to be known by the word *bourgeois,* which was really much better suited to the inhabitants of the old burgs, at the foot of which they settled, is to be found in the fact that very early the mercantile group too surrounded itself by a wall or palisade for the sake of security, and thus became a burg in its turn. This extension of meaning is all the more easily comprehensible, since the new burg very soon overshadowed the old. In the most active centres of commercial life, such as Bruges, it was already at the beginning of the twelfth century surrounding the fortress, which had been its nucleus, on all sides. The accessory had become the essential, the new-comers had triumphed over the old inhabitants. In this sense it is strictly true to say that the medieval town, and consequently the modern town, had its birth in the faubourg of the city, or of the bourg which determined its site.

The collection of merchants in favourable spots soon caused artisans also to collect there. Industrial concentration is as old as commercial concentration. We can observe it with particular plainness in Flanders. Clothmaking, which had at first been carried on in the country, emigrated of itself to places which offered a sale for its products. There weavers found wool imported by the merchants, fullers' and dyers' soap and dye-stuffs. A real industrial revolution, of which we do not, unfortunately, know the details, accompanied this transformation of a rural industry into an urban one. . . .

II. THE MERCHANTS AND THE BOURGEOISIE

The essential difference between the merchants and artisans of the nascent towns and the agricultural society in the midst of which they appeared, was that their kind of life was no longer determined by their relations with the land. In this respect they formed, in every sense of the word, a class of *déracinés.* Commerce and industry, which up till then had been merely the adventitious or intermittent occupations of manorial agents, whose existence was assured by the great landowners who employed them, now became independent professions. Those who practised them were incontestably "new men." Attempts have often been made to derive them from the servile personnel attached to the domestic workshops of the manor, or the serfs who were charged with feeding the household in times of scarcity and in time of plenty disposed of their surplus production outside. But such an evolution is neither supported by the sources nor probable. There is no doubt that territorial lords here and there preserved economic prerogatives in the nascent towns for a fairly long time, such prerogatives, for instance, as the obligation of the burgesses to use the lord's oven and mill, the monopoly of sale enjoyed by his wine for several days after the vintage, or even certain dues levied from the craft gilds. But the local survival of these rights is no proof of the manorial origin of urban economy. On the contrary, what we note everywhere is that from the moment that it appears, it appears in a condition of freedom.

But the question immediately occurs, how are we to explain the formation of a class of free merchants and artisans in the midst of an exclusively rural society, where serfdom was the normal condition of the people? Scarcity of information prevents us from replying with that precision which the importance of the problem demands, but it is at least possible to indicate the chief factors. First, it is incontestable that commerce and industry were originally recruited from among landless men, who lived, so to speak, on the margin of a society where land alone was the basis of existence. Now these men were very numerous. Apart altogether from those, who in times of famine or war left their native soil to seek a livelihood elsewhere and returned no more, we have to remember all the individuals whom the manorial organisation itself was unable to support. The peasants' holdings were of such a size as to secure the regular payment of the dues assessed upon them. Thus the younger sons of a man overburdened with children were often forced to leave their father in order to enable him to make his payments to the lord. Thenceforth they swelled the crowd of vagabonds who roamed through the country, going from abbey to abbey taking their share of alms reserved for the poor, hiring themselves out to the peasants at harvest time or at the vintage, and enlisting as mercenaries in the feudal troops in times of war.

These men were quick to profit by the new means of livelihood offered them by the arrival of ships and merchants along the coasts and in the river estuaries. Many of the more adventurous certainly hired themselves to the Venetian and Scandinavian boats as sailors; others joined the merchant caravans which took their way more and more frequently to the "ports." With luck, the best among them could not fail to seize the many opportunities of making a fortune, which commercial life offered to the vagabonds and adventurers who threw themselves into it with energy and intelligence. Strong probability would suffice to support such a reconstruction of the facts, even if we did not possess, in the story of St. Godric of Finchale, a valuable example of the way in which the *nouveaux riches* were then formed.[1] Godric was born towards the end of the eleventh century in Lincolnshire of poor peasant stock and, forced, no doubt, to leave his parents' holding, he must have had to use all his wits to get a living. Like many other unfortunates in every age he became a beachcomber, on the look-out for wreckage thrown up by the waves. Shipwrecks were numerous and one fine day a lucky chance furnished him with a windfall which enabled him to get together a pedlar's pack. He had amassed a little store of money, when he met with and joined a band of merchants. Their business prospered and he soon made enough profit to enable him to form a partnership with others, in common with whom he loaded a ship and engaged in coastal trade along the shores of England, Scotland, Flanders and Denmark. The partnership prospered. Its operations consisted in taking abroad goods which were known to be scarce there and bringing back a return cargo, which was then exported to places where the demand was greatest and where, in consequence, the largest profits could be realised.

The story of Godric was certainly that of many others. In an age when local famines were continual, one had only to buy a very small quantity of grain cheaply in regions where it was abundant, to realise fabulous profits, which could then be increased by the same methods. Thus speculation, which is the starting-point in this kind of business, largely contributed to the foundation of the first commercial fortunes. The savings of a little pedlar, a sailor, a boatman, or a docker, furnished him with quite enough capital, if only he knew how to use it. It might also happen that a landowner would invest a part of his income in maritime commerce. It is almost certain that the nobles on the Ligurian coast advanced the necessary funds to build the Genoese ships and shared in the profits from the sale of cargoes in the Mediterranean ports. The same thing must have happened in other Italian cities; at least we are tempted to assume so when we observe that in Italy a large proportion of the nobility always lived in the cities, in contrast to their brothers north of the Alps. It is only natural to suppose that a certain number of them were in some way interested in the economic revival which was developing around them. In these cases landed capital unquestionably contributed to the formation of liquid capital. However, their share was secondary, and though they profited by the recovery of trade, it was certainly not they who revived it.

The first impetus started from outside, in the South with Venetian and in the North

[1] Translated by G. G. Coulton, *Social Life in Britain* (Cambridge, England, 1918), pp. 415–420. [Editor's note.]

with Scandinavian navigation. Western Europe, crystallised in its agricultural civilisation, could not of itself have become so rapidly acquainted with a new sort of life, in the absence of external stimulus and example. The attitude of the Church, the most powerful landowner of the time, towards commerce, an attitude not merely passive but actively hostile, is quite enough proof of that. If the first beginnings of commercial capitalism partly evade our notice, it is much easier to follow its evolution during the course of the twelfth century. In the vigour and relative rapidity of its development it may, without exaggeration, be compared with the industrial revolution of the nineteenth century. The new kind of life which offered itself to the roving masses of landless men had an irresistible attraction for them, by reason of the promise of gain which it offered. The result was a real emigration from the country to the nascent towns. Soon, it was not only vagabonds of the type of Godric who bent their steps thither. The temptation was too great not to cause a number of serfs to run away from the manors where they were born and settle in the towns, either as artisans or as employees of the rich merchants whose reputation spread through the land. The lords pursued them and brought them back to their holdings, when they succeeded in laying hands on them. But many eluded their search, and as the city population increased, it became dangerous to try to seize the fugitives under its protection. . . .

III. URBAN INSTITUTIONS AND LAW

The needs and tendencies of the bourgeoisie were so incompatible with the traditional organisation of Western Europe that they immediately aroused violent opposition. They ran counter to all the interests and ideas of a society dominated materially by the owners of large landed property and spiritually by the Church, whose aversion to trade was unconquerable. It would be unfair to attribute to "feudal tyranny" or "sacerdotal arrogance" an opposition which explains itself, although the attribution has often been made. As always, those who were the beneficiaries of the established order defended it obstinately, not only because it guaranteed their interests, but because it seemed to them indispensable to the preservation of society. Moreover, the bourgeois themselves were far from taking up a revolutionary attitude towards this society. They took for granted the authority of the territorial princes, the privileges of the nobility and, above all, those of the Church. They even professed an ascetic morality, which was plainly contradicted by their mode of life. They merely desired a place in the sun, and their claims were confined to their most indispensable needs.

Of the latter, the most indispensable was personal liberty. Without liberty, that is to say, without the power to come and go, to do business, to sell goods, a power not enjoyed by serfdom, trade would be impossible. Thus they claimed it, simply for the advantages which it conferred, and nothing was further from the mind of the bourgeoisie than any idea of freedom as a natural right; in their eyes it was merely a useful one. Besides, many of them possessed it *de facto;* they were immigrants, who had come from too far off for their lord to be traced and who, since their serfdom could not be presumed, necessarily passed for free, although born of unfree parents. But the fact had to be transformed into a right. It was essential that the villeins, who came to settle in the towns to seek a new livelihood, should feel safe and should not have to fear being taken back by force to the manors from which they had escaped. They must be delivered from labour services and from all the hated dues by which the servile population was burdened, such as the obligation to marry only a woman of their own class and to leave to the lord part of their inheritance. Willy-nilly, in the course of the twelfth century these claims, backed up as they often were by dangerous revolts, had to be granted. The most obstinate conservatives, such as

Guibert de Nogent, in 1115, were reduced to a wordy revenge, speaking of those "detestable communes" which the serfs had set up to escape from their lord's authority and to do away with his most lawful rights.[2] Freedom became the legal status of the bourgeoisie, so much so that it was no longer a personal privilege only, but a territorial one, inherent in urban soil just as serfdom was in manorial soil. In order to obtain it, it was enough to have resided for a year and a day within the walls of the town. "City air makes a man free" (*Stadtluft macht frei*), says the German proverb.

But if liberty was the first need of the burgess, there were many others besides. Traditional law with its narrow, formal procedure, its ordeals, its judicial duels, its judges recruited from among the rural population, and knowing no other custom than that which had been gradually elaborated to regulate the relations of men living by the cultivation or the ownership of the land, was inadequate for a population whose existence was based on commerce and industry. A more expeditious law was necessary, means of proof more rapid and more independent of chance, and judges who were themselves acquainted with the professional occupations of those who came under their jurisdiction, and could cut short their arguments by a knowledge of the case at issue. Very early, and at latest at the beginning of the eleventh century, the pressure of circumstances led to the creation of a *jus mercatorum,* i.e., an embryonic commercial code. It was a collection of usages born of business experience, a sort of international custom, which the merchants used among themselves in their transactions. Devoid of all legal validity, it was impossible to invoke it in the existing law courts, so the merchants agreed to choose among themselves arbitrators who had the necessary competence to understand their disputes and to settle them promptly. It is here undoubtedly that we must seek the origin of those law courts, which in England received the picturesque name of courts of *piepowder* (*pied poudré*), because the feet of the merchants who resorted to them were still dusty from the roads.[3] Soon this *ad hoc* jurisdiction became permanent and was recognised by public authority. At Ypres, in 1116, the Count of Flanders abolished the judicial duel, and it is certain that about the same date he instituted in most of his towns local courts of *échevins,* chosen from among the burgesses and alone competent to judge them. Sooner or later the same thing happened in all countries. In Italy, France, Germany and England the towns obtained judicial autonomy, which made them islands of independent jurisdiction, lying outside the territorial custom.

This jurisdictional autonomy was accompanied by administrative autonomy. The formation of urban agglomerations entailed a number of arrangements for convenience of defence, which they had to provide for themselves in the absence of the traditional authorities, who had neither the means nor the wish to help them. It is a strong testimony to the energy and the initiative of the bourgeoisie that it succeeded by its own efforts in setting on foot the municipal organisation, of which the first outlines appear in the eleventh century, and which was already in possession of all its essential organs in the twelfth. The work thus accomplished is all the more admirable because it was an original creation. There was nothing in the existing order of things to serve it as a model, since the needs it was designed to meet were new.

The most pressing was the need for defence. The merchants and their merchandise were, indeed, such a tempting prey that it was essential to protect them from pillagers by a strong wall. The construction of ramparts was thus the first public work undertaken by the towns and one which, down to the end of the Middle Ages, was their heaviest financial burden.

[2] *The Autobiography of Guibert, Abbot of Nogent-sous-Coucy* (London, 1925), pp. 153–154. [Editor's note.]

[3] See below, pp. 94–96. [Editor's note.]

Indeed, it may be truly said to have been the starting-point of their financial organisation, whence, for example, the name of *firmitas,* by which the communal tax was always known at Liége, and the appropriation in a number of cities *ad opus castri* (i.e., for the improvement of the fortifications) of a part of the fines imposed by the borough court. The fact that today municipal coats of arms are surrounded by a walled crown shows the importance accorded to the ramparts. There were no unfortified towns in the Middle Ages.

Money had to be raised to provide for the expenses occasioned by the permanent need for fortifications, and it could be raised most easily from the burgesses themselves. All were interested in the common defence and all were obliged to meet the cost. The quota payable by each was calculated on the basis of his fortune. This was a great innovation. For the arbitrary seigneurial tallage, collected in the sole interest of the lord, it substituted a payment proportionate to the means of the taxpayer and set apart for an object of general utility. Thus taxation recovered its public character, which had disappeared during the feudal era. To assess and collect this tax, as well as to provide for the ordinary necessities whose numbers grew with the constant increase of the town population, the establishment of quays and markets, the building of bridges and parish churches, the regulation of crafts and the supervision of food supplies, it soon became necessary to elect or allow the setting up of a council of magistrates, consuls in Italy and Provence, *jurés* in France and aldermen in England.[4] . . .

The essential characteristic of the bourgeoisie was, indeed, the fact that it formed a privileged class in the midst of the rest of the population. From this point of view the medieval town offers a striking contrast both to the ancient town and to the town of today, which are differentiated only by the density of their population and their complex administration; apart from this, neither in public nor in private law do their inhabitants occupy a peculiar position in the State. The medieval burgess, on the contrary, was a different kind of person from all who lived outside the town walls. Once outside the gates and the moat we are in another world, or more exactly, in the domain of another law. The acquisition of citizenship brought with it results analogous to those which followed when a man was dubbed knight or a clerk tonsured, in the sense that they conferred a peculiar legal status. Like the clerk or the noble, the burgess escaped from the common law; like them, he belonged to a particular estate (*status*), which was later to be known as the "third estate."

[4] Below, pp. 65–66. [Editor's note.]

Towns Create Commerce

LEWIS MUMFORD

Lewis Mumford (1895–), is America's most prolific and honored writer on cultural history, architecture, city-planning, literature and the human condition. Although he studied at the City College of New York, Columbia University and the New School for Social Research (under Thorstein Veblen), Mumford never bothered to obtain an academic degree, and he has spent most of his life "not in finding or fabricating the pieces but in putting them together into a significant picture." The study of cities, their planning, buildings, history and effects upon human beings has appeared repeatedly in his twenty books. In 1962 his *The City in History* received the National Book Award for nonfiction, and in 1963 he became president of the American Academy of Arts and Letters. The following excerpt from *The City in History* begins with the effects of the barbarian invasions of the Roman world.

BECAUSE OF a wealth of literary evidence, we have a better picture of what went on in Gaul than elsewhere. And there is no doubt that the cities that managed to fortify themselves against the barbarians occupied a much smaller area than they had previously spread over. Bordeaux was reduced by its walls to a third of its previous size, and Autun, founded by Augustus, shrank from a town of five hundred acres to a village of twenty-five.

We have an even fuller picture of what happened from Nîmes and Arles, in Provence. In Nîmes the old amphitheater was transformed by the Visigoths into a little town, with two thousand inhabitants and two churches: after closing the entrances to the theater, the heavy masonry walls served as ramparts. And though the walls of Arles had been rebuilt by Theodoric, they were ruined again in the struggle between Charles Martel and the Arabs: after which the amphitheater at Arles, too, served as fortress, and a small medieval town grew up within it, more crowded than most, as a seventeenth-century print still shows us; for the buildings of this little settlement were not destroyed till the beginning of the nineteenth century. . . .

If the Saracen encirclement of the Mediterranean hastened the passage from the uniform imperial organization to an economy of local production and barter, with a crazy-quilt of local customs, local laws, conflicting jurisdictions, the final blow came from the other end of Europe in the invasions of the Norsemen in the ninth century. The final blow — and the first move toward recovery. These berserk raids were conducted in small boats that pierced to the heart of the countryside between Brittany and the Elbe; no district was immune to their sacking, burning, slaying. Apprehension over such forays may have created a new bond of interest between the feudal chieftain and his tributary peasants. But it also showed the technical inferiority of the scattered local war bands rallying on foot in opposing attacks carried out by swift-moving sea lords, specialized in war.

Sheer necessity led to the rediscovery of that ancient urban safeguard, the wall. Against sudden raids a wall, on guard at all hours, was more useful than any amount of military courage. The strength and security of a stronghold perched on a steep rock could be reproduced even in the lowlands, provided the inhabitants of a village built a masonry wall, or even a wooden palisade. . . .

In terror of the invaders, the inhabitants of Mainz, for example, at last restored their broken Roman walls. And under commissions from the German Emperor Henry I, walls were built even around monasteries and nunneries to guard them from pagan attack. Twice in the ninth century, in 860 and 878, the monastery of St. Omer had been devastated by the Norsemen. But when these Vikings returned in 891, they found that the Abbey had at last erected walls and could defy them. So successful indeed was this renewed mode of achieving security that, by the tenth century, the monastery of St. Omer had become a town.

As early as 913 the "Anglo-Saxon Chronicle" reports further that the building of fortresses and of walls around settlements was one of the chief activities of the King's army.[1] Here is still further evidence, if any be needed, of the role of kings as city builders, through their ability to mobilize extra labor. But even as early as 885 the "Chronicle" shows, Rochester was walled and successfully defended by its burghers;

[1] Below, p. 51. [Editor's note.]

while a year later King Alfred himself fortified the city of London.[2] Military service became a necessity of citizenship, and it is even possible that the ability to provide a permanent army and to repair walls around a town was, as Frederick William Maitland suggests, one of the qualifications for corporate urban franchise.

The walled enclosure not merely gave protection from outside invasion: it had a new political function, for it proved a double-edged instrument. Reversing the ancient city's precedent, the wall could be used to maintain freedom within. By means of the wall, a little town, once helpless before even a small armed force, would become a stronghold. People would flock to such blessed islands of peace, as originally they had submitted in desperation to feudal gangleaders, becoming their vassals and serfs in return for a bit of land and security — or had given up all hopes of domestic felicity to find a sterile sanctuary in a monastery or a nunnery.

There was safety, once the wall was erected, in numbers. Life in the isolated countryside, even under the shadow of a nearby castle, now ceased to be as attractive as life in the populated town. Labor on the wall itself was a cheap price to pay for such security and regularity in trade and work. Though the right to build walls remained, significantly, a royal prerogative, the Peace of Constance, in 1184, yielded this right to the free cities of Italy.

Note the sequence. First the cowering countryside, with its local production and its mainly local barter. Only the abbeys and the royal estates would exchange their wine, their grain, their oil, over great distances. What trade came to a town from a distance was fitful and unreliable. But once a town was encircled by a wall, other normal attributes of urban life would appear: the container, reestablished, became also a magnet. The extension of the wall from the castle or the abbey to the neighboring village often marked the physical beginning of a town, though the full legal privileges of an active municipal corporation could be obtained only by hard bargaining with the Bishop or the feudal proprietor who held the land.

The greatest economic privilege, that of holding a regular market once a week, assembling for exchange the neighboring peasants, fishermen, craftsmen, depended upon both physical security and legal sanctuary. So, as in ancient Greece, those who came to market were protected, during the marketing hours, by the Market Peace, now symbolized by the market cross of the marketplace. Here a new class got protection against theft and arbitrary tribute, and began to settle down permanently, at first just outside the walls: the merchants. When they became permanent members of the town corporation, a new era began, which helped reopen the old highways and waterways.

The fact that the merchants represented a new class can be deduced from their topographic position in the newly laid out "suburb" just outside the walls. If at first the castle or the monastery was the town center, after the eleventh century the fresh activities of the community began to shift toward the marketplace, and the incorporation of merchants and craftsmen, as free citizens, would be marked in more than one place by the extension of the wall around their suburb. It is significant to note that . . . the *new* quarter in Regensburg in the eleventh century — as distinguished from the royal and clerical quarters — was that of the traders. . . .

Sometimes urbanization was deliberately promoted by feudal lords, seeking to increase their income by utilizing urban ground rents, taking a share of the tolls at the local market, making use of a big body of consumers to increase the value of the products of their own estates, not consumable on the premises. Often the demand by the towns for independence was opposed by the feudal proprietors: particularly by the Bishops, who were more formidable than war-chiefs because they were agents of a wide-flung institution, commanding both material and spiritual re-

[2] Below, p. 50. [Editor's note.]

sources of an unusual kind. In some countries, as in England and France, municipal freedom was promoted by a temporary coalition with the central power, as a means of weakening the feudal nobles who challenged the king's dominion. But, opposed or helped, the population flowed into these protected centers, built and rebuilt them, and brought neglected parts of their life to a new pitch of activity and productiveness. In a few centuries, the cities of Europe recaptured much of the ground the disintegration of the Roman Empire had lost.

The revival of trade is often taken, even by excellent scholars like Pirenne, as the direct cause of the city building and civilizing activities that took place in the eleventh century. But before this could happen, a surplus of rural products and a surplus of population were necessary, to provide both goods for trade and customers to purchase them. If the merchants themselves had been the chief occupants of the new cities, they would have had to take in each other's washing. . . .

Happily, the holding of a regular market in a protected place worked to the advantage of the feudal lord or monastic proprietor. Considerably before the grand revival of trade in the eleventh century, one finds under Otto II (973–983) that permission was given to the widow Imma, who was founding a cloister in Kärnten, to provide a market and a mint, and to draw taxes therefrom: typical provisions in much later charters for new cities. In the time of Otto . . . most of the market privileges were granted to religious proprietors, rather than to temporal lords. . . .

But note: the regular market, held once or sometimes twice a week, under the protection of Bishop or Abbot, was an instrument of local life, not of international trade. So it should be no surprise that as early as 833, when long-distance trade was mostly in abeyance, Lewis the Pious in Germany gave a monastery permission to erect a mint for a market already in existence. The revival of trade in the eleventh century, then, was not the critical event that laid the foundations of the new medieval type of city: as I have shown, many new urban foundations antedate that fact, and more evidence could be added. Commercial zeal was rather a symptom of a more inclusive revival that was taking place in Western civilization: and that was partly a mark of the new sense of security that the walled town itself had helped to bring into existence. . . .

The over-emphasis of the role of the market as a generator of towns derives partly from the fact that historians have read present motives and incentives back into past situations; and partly it comes from their failure to distinguish the different roles of local, regional, and international markets. This whole development was misconstrued by Pirenne because he refused the title of city to an urban community that did not foster long-distance trade and harbor a large mercantile middle class — a quite arbitrary definition.

International markets have little effect upon the founding of towns. Great international fairs in the Middle Ages often took place at the time of a religious festival, when pilgrims from many parts of the country would flock to a holy shrine: it was the concourse of pilgrims that would draw travelling merchants temporarily to such a spot. But such fairs occurred, at most, only four times a year; and when the pilgrims went away, the merchants departed, too. Such international trade was too limited to keep a city going throughout a year: indeed, we know from the late example of Nizhni Novgorod that the city that mushroomed around the fair would be almost deserted the rest of the year. International trade did not produce medieval cities: but it promoted their growth, as at Venice, Genoa, Milan, Arras, Bruges, after they had been established for other purposes.

In general, the reason for the trader's secondary role should be plain: trade revival on capitalistic lines was confined to luxury wares, drawn from every part of Europe and even, after the Crusades, from the East. But the town itself was a place of exchange for local agricultural and handicraft production: so that even at a later period than the eleventh century, the merchants with their retainers accounted . . . for only a small part of the town's population. However important commerce became, it was the producers in the medieval town that composed about four-fifths of the inhabitants, as compared with perhaps one-fifth or less in the present-day city. . . .

The truth, then, lies in just the opposite interpretation to Pirenne's: it was the revival of the protected town that helped the reopening of the regional and international trade routes, and led to the trans-European circulation of surplus commodities, particularly those luxuries that could be sold at a high profit to the princes and magnates, or those articles in sufficiently short local supply to command good prices: fine wool from England, wine from the Rhine, spices and silks from the East, armor from Lombardy, saffron and quicksilver from Spain, leather from Pomerania, finished textiles from Flanders, not least religious icons and devotional objects from various art centers.

Cities formed the stepping-stones in this march of goods: from Byzantium to Venice, from Venice to Augsburg, and over the Rhine; and so, too, from Marseille and Bordeaux to Lyons and Paris, or from the Baltic towns like Dantzig and Stralsund down to the Mediterranean. The famous marzipan of Lübeck testifies by both its name (St. Mark's Bread) and its composition (almonds and rose water) to this relationship with Venice and the East. With this passage of goods, cities established first on a basis of local production grew in population and wealth; and the merchant population naturally grew with them.

The Variety of Urban Development

EDITH ENNEN

Edith Ennen (1907–), author of the leading postwar study of the early history of European towns, *Frühgeschichte der europäischen Stadt* (1953), combines the scope of an historian with an archivist's sense of precision and documentation. After taking her doctorate at the University of Bonn, she worked during World War II at the Institute for the Historical Regional Study of the Rheinland; in 1947 she became director of the city archives of Bonn; in 1961 she accepted a professorial post at the University of Bonn; and in 1964 she was named Professor of Economic and Social History at the university of her native Saarland. The following article is an expansion of a paper presented to the Tenth International Congress of the Historical Sciences at Rome in 1955. In it Professor Ennen treats typology in the technical sense given to the word in English by archaeology, as the classification of materials according to the type they exhibit and its evolution.

A HISTORICAL TYPOLOGY of medieval towns must take account of all the forms of urban life and of the conditions in which they were born. Topography, social structure, the multiple functions of the town as an economic, administrative, or religious center, and legal and constitutional institutions considered in their recip-

From Edith Ennen, "Les différents types de formation des villes européennes," *Le Moyen Age,* vol. LXII (1956), pp. 397–411, with footnotes omitted. Reprinted by permission of the publisher and emendations graciously supplied by the author. Translated by the editor.

rocal relations and their mutual interdependence constitute types to be grasped and understood as the product of a concrete historical situation.

To take account of the extraordinary development characteristic of medieval town life, it is necessary to recognize the diversity of conditions at the very beginning of medieval European towns, to evaluate the early conflicting forces at work in the Romano-Germanic settings, and to determine the impulses and influences which appeared in the midst of these two cultures. Within the vast area of Europe, numerous subspecies of urban forms were created, due sometimes to the variations and mixing of the principal types of towns, sometimes to different regional and chronological combinations, and finally sometimes to outside influences or chance. We cannot study these distinctions here in all their forms.

The initial difference results from the relationship of the medieval to the ancient town. The fall of ancient civilization has often been considered a dramatic catastrophe, brought on by the invasion of the Germanic "barbarians" or by that of the Arabs, who are said to have cut off the Mediterranean. At the present such a view has been abandoned in favor of the opinion, now more generally accepted, that there was in fact a gradual transition between Rome and the middle ages. With respect to the nature of this transition and to its interpretation, a scholarly discussion developed which attempts to give more and more precise delineation to historical events. This circumstance has taught us to make the necessary chronological and regional distinctions; we have also hoped to achieve greater precision not only by considering the urban phenomenon in its complexity, but by dissecting it into its constitutive elements in order to be able to follow separately the study of the disappearance and the survival of various urban functions.

In regard to the continuity of civilization, three different regions of town life can be distinguished in Europe: (1) the north German area, to the east of the Rhine and in Scandinavia, which was not directly influenced by the urban culture of the Mediterranean, (2) the zone which corresponds to nothern France and the valleys of the Rhine and the Danube, where the remains of the towns of antiquity disappeared to a large degree, but not without leaving some evident traces (pre-Norman England, where a minimum of ancient survivals have been noted, is closely attached to the north German area), and (3) the southern regions where Roman urban traditions continued with respect to the possession of the land, housing, and manner of life. In Italy, economic and social development continued without a break, as has recently been shown for the Po valley. There is no argument about the basic continuity here of the legal form of the urban community. On the other hand, in the second zone mentioned above — Gaul, and the regions of the Rhine and the Danube — as well as in Spain and in the south of France, the disappearance of Roman municipal organization is a certain fact.

Obviously, most of the problems are posed by the towns of the intermediate region, and this region itself contains its differences. On its borders, that is, on the Lower Rhine and along the Danube, the collapse of municipal life was quite marked, while in the lands of the Moselle and the middle Rhine the classical urban heritage was better preserved. Much more than the Franks, the Alamanni made a clean sweep of the past, as appears from the examples of the *civitates* of the upper Rhine and Switzerland.

If one looks into how those functions which were specifically urban were maintained in this intermediate zone, important differences in degree are again apparent. The old Roman municipal organization disappeared completely, as has been said. Towns as such did not continue as essential organs of the public life of the State, and the countryside acquired its own political significance. In the Carolingian period the ancient *civitates* were the residences of administrators or sovereigns only to a very limited degree. From the economic point of view certain technical activities, such as pottery or glassmaking, still continued. But the industrial organization peculiar to the Roman period disappeared. For the greater part of the time, manorialism replaced the town; probably it gave life to the Frankish pottery workshops which exported their goods in bulk as far as Scandinavia, and which we find in the *Vorgebirge* between Bonn and Cologne. This industry did not, however, fall to the level of a simple household activity.

We owe our knowledge of these workshops and their export business to archaeologists, and we must also turn to them for help if we wish to study the continuity of dwelling-sites. This latter problem is one which only local research can clarify for each particular use. Indeed, it is necessary to examine things very clearly: even when the area of habitation within a town appears at first glance to offer an example of complete continuity, shifts of the center of gravity in this area can often be determined. For example, one can see at Bonn a shift something like that of a pendulum between the site of the Roman station (outside the medieval wall at the north of the present town) and the nucleus of the medieval town, located five-eighths of a mile to the south in the region of the Christian martyrs of the late Empire and of the shrines which were erected there. The case of Bonn, which is far from unique, has a great historical and methodological importance, for thanks to it Aubin[1] was the first to be able to describe the phenomenon of the shift of the center of gravity of a town.

That the site of the tombs of the first Christian martyrs of the late Empire should become the embryo of a medieval town is a very characteristic thing and is explained by a factor which was the decisive element in the transition between antiquity and the middle ages: the Christian Church. Since 1930 excavations made first at Bonn and Xanten, then at Cologne and Trier, and more recently at Boppard on the Rhine have revealed the importance of the Christian communities of the Rhineland at the end of antiquity. We owe to the archaeologist Kempf and to the historian Ewig our knowledge of the situation at Trier. The episcopal church of this town at the time of Constantine has been revealed as a double church, which in its height and surface area can be compared to the largest religious buildings of early Christianity. It could shelter a Christian community amounting to several thousand people. From Trier, in fact, the ecclesiastical organization of the Rhineland took its start about 250. This was apparently the time of Eucharius, who was, according to the most reliable episcopal lists of the tenth century, the first head of the Church in the region of the Moselle. These episcopal lists from Trier contain no gaps and prove in a positive fashion that ecclesiastical organization survived the Germanic invasions, at the same time that the shrines and Christian communities held their ground.

The Church of the Martyrs at Bonn also survived the invasions, and the continuation of a Roman provincial population along with the conquering Franks is shown by the excavations made at the cemeteries of Andernach and Bonn by K. Böhner. Thanks to the presence of Christian communities, not only technical knowledge and the remains of dwelling-places were preserved; there remained also a certain spiritual force, although it did not contain all or even, as some would have it, the essential part of the classical heritage. All the same, in the shadow of the church many urban traditions were maintained: the habit of living in common (a practice which was then adopted by the clergy), the use of writing for all cultural expressions, the role of the town as a center of worship and of ecclesiastical organization. But in these various matters a setback can be seen in the Carolingian era, which shows

[1] Hermann Aubin (1885–), Professor Emeritus of the University of Hamburg, now at Freiburg in Breisgau. [Editor's note.]

a greater contrast with antiquity than the Merovingian period, as Pirenne pointed out. From then on the use of writing became the special province of the clergy, and lay education disappeared; likewise, ecclesiastical centers independent of urban episcopal sees were reestablished in isolated abbeys and in a constantly increasing number of rural churches.

Nevertheless, episcopal organization, with its peculiarly urban ability to preserve and to create, and the attraction which centers of worship exercised on the population, were phenomena common to all Europe. The residence of a bishop gave to towns — including those of the Rhineland as well as the Roman cities of the old province of Narbonne — such an importance that even at the lowest point of decay of the urban economy they always prevailed over manorial centers. Such residence also explains how in the valleys of the Meuse (Liège) and of the Rhône the *villa* was raised to the rank of *civitas*.

To the initial differentiation in the history of towns was added the play of opposing forces at the very moment of their origin. Towns were not known in the northern German zone, where the population was scattered and the class of great manorial lords dominated. Nevertheless, in what is called a *wik*, that is, a base of operations for itinerant merchants organized in professional associations, this zone possessed an original element which prefigured urban life. In the intermediate zone where the Roman urban tradition was partially preserved, these *wiks* acquired an importance which would be decisive for the origin of the medieval town. Indeed, they could combine with the *civitates* of Roman origin and the castles in a fashion which would be fruitful. Beside the *castrum* [military camp] of Regensburg formed the *pagus mercatorum* [mercantile district]. Before the ruined walls of *Colonia Claudia Agrippensium*,[2] the suburb of the merchants of Cologne developed along the Rhine. On the right bank of the Meuse facing the episcopal town clinging to the steep rocky bank opposite, the *negotiatorum oppidum* [fortification of the merchants] of the rich slave merchants of Verdun was born. Before the count's castle at Ghent the *portus* of the *viri hereditarii* [mercantile settlement of hereditary proprietors] was established. This topographical and constitutional duality, which was special to the towns of northwest Europe from their beginning, has been particularly studied and emphasized by Belgian and German historians. Recently it has been possible to be more precise about this occurrence by delineating the respective roles in the creation of the town which fell to the unfortified merchant colony and to the lord's castle. It has also been possible to measure the degree of change of these two essential elements of formation: one evolved from the episcopal residence inside a Roman town to the dynastic castle; the other changed from a colony of merchants devoted to long-distance commerce into a market for artisans. Indeed, alongside the "commercial renaissance" one can see in northwest Europe the birth of the cloth industry, which gave rise to a precocious export trade. These two economic phenomena were favored by a considerable increase in the population and an extension of its distribution.

The proportional strength of the *civitas* and the *wik* thus varies profoundly. The following rule can be rigorously formulated: the farther north one goes the more the importance of the *civitas* decreases, while that of the *wik* increases. Thus, for example, in the towns of western Europe the majority of the churches are collegiate churches[3] or abbeys, while in the northern towns the churches are the creations of merchant associations. In these latter towns individuals who practiced export trade determined the religious life, while in western Europe the churches were often older

[2] Roman name of Cologne, established as a colony by the Emperor Claudius, at the request of his wife, Agrippina. [Editor's note.]

[3] Those served by a "college" of canons. [Editor's note.]

than the merchant colony. The formation of towns in the northwest of Europe, therefore, resulted from a process of fusion and penetration; traveling merchants became traders resident in the town and, imitating the residence of the lord, they used a stone wall to defend the *wik*. At the time of the formation of the commune the forces of association represented by the merchants' gilds, the legally free communities and others, as well as the associations bound by oath, gained the victory.

In the northwest of continental Europe the political autonomy of the countryside held its position, as did the seigneurial organization of society, reflected by the existence of castles which the nobles possessed outside of the towns.

We have already noted the regional differences which may be observed within this general type — for instance, the different proportions which exist between the *civitas* and *wik* and the respective variations which these two elements present. A very special evolution may, however, be noted in England. While on the continent the towns were organisms foreign to the manorial economy which surrounded them, in England the state and the manor were very early oriented towards a money economy. This was a consequence of the conquest of the island by the Normans, since they were men given to commerce and calculation. The influence of the money economy in the organization of the state is shown by the precocious appearance of an exchequer with an improved system of record-keeping and the intervention of the state with respect to money, weights and measures. Manorial lords in England made use of the same precise procedures as the state administration for the recording of revenue. The systematic limitation of seigneurial justice by the king and the disappearance of the baronial revenues which resulted from it prompted the barons to direct their activity toward economic enterprises. The role of income in the English manorial economy led to renting, the more easily since the exceptionally good road system favored small ventures. Thus land became a commodity. The landlords of the county participated in the activities of the urban merchant gilds. The consequence of this intervention of the merchant gilds in the rural life of the county was that in England the concept of business did not rest on a narrow base limited to the territory of the towns. To this may be added the fact that insofar as the English nobility constituted a "class" it was not closed to the urban bourgeoisie, and the younger sons of the families of the higher nobility entered the gentry.

Just as the English towns seen from the economic point of view showed relatively little difference from the countryside, so also, considered as organisms established on the basis of association, they did not follow the continental pattern of isolation in the midst of a basically seigneurial setting, precisely because of the development of the English county in the direction of autonomous organization. Here feudalism had not completely destroyed the popular legal support of the monarchy. At the county court held in the presence of a royal itinerant justice, landlords, clergy and representatives of the towns and village communities came together. Thus Parliament was already prefigured, so to speak, in the county court. The towns felt no need to claim autonomy, and the political forces which therefore remained available were concentrated in the Parliament. The towns retained only a limited autonomy; on the other hand, Parliament created a union among the borough communities.

The towns of the Mediterranean, markedly different from the towns of northwest Europe, appear as a particular type of medieval urban civilization. In Italy they attained their most remarkable manifestation. From the beginning towns had existed in this country. The dualism characteristic of the urban plans of northwest Europe contrasts with the unity of the *civitas* in Italy. Towns there were both communities whose inhabitants were primarily attached to an agricultural economy, and the starting-places of regional markets; in the high middle ages, as early as the tenth century, the towns of Italy and Spain obtained the privilege of asylum and immunity granted in the form characteristic of medieval law. In their social hierarchy rigorous distinctions based on birth were not known. Already in the ninth and tenth centuries free merchants, whose continuing presence has been established, were acquiring lands in the *contado* [surrounding countryside]. Whether they liked it or not, the nobility settled in the towns. The residence of the nobility in the towns became one of the characteristics of the Mediterranean urban type. In the towns of Italy, Spain, and southern France, towers inhabited by nobles sprang up everywhere. Thanks to the residence agreements which the town of Genoa, for example, concluded on a large scale with the nobility established about the city, the *contado* was deprived of its governing class and became a territory directed by the town itself. Thus the urban republics of northern Italy, which were above all merchant city-states, were born. They prevented the formation of states organized on a territorial base and in terms of a hierarchy of social classes, like the German principalities and the French monarchy as early as 1200. Italy thus developed a class of wealthy men among whom differences due to birth were obliterated. While in the north itinerant merchants became townsmen, in the south urban landlords became merchants.

If the process of development of medieval towns brings out a clear opposition between north and south, it shows nevertheless that there was often a fusion of the materials from which the towns were formed and the factors which produced them, and that there were also strong reciprocal influences between these different factors. The classical heritage did not remain localized in the regions where it was best preserved; it was also transmitted to the countries of northern Europe. The fashion of living in groups and the practice of building in stone, necessary conditions for the birth of towns, moved from the south to the north. Today the type of dwelling suited to the southern regions can still be seen in the valleys of the Meuse, the upper Moselle, the Saar, and the Rhone, for these are the traditional routes of the influence of Mediterranean civilization. It is apparent in the large villages of Lorraine, distinguished by their stone houses with flat roofs, and in the villages squeezed between the mountains of Valais in Switzerland, where the fields are enclosed by stone walls and not by hedges or wooden fences. What a strange and characteristically urban impression is created by Namur, a mass of houses and stone buildings closed in by the rock wall, the Sambre, and the Meuse, while an hour's drive away the great town of Brussels, the capital of Belgium, gradually spreads into the suburbs and the rural landscape of Brabant.

From the Mediterranean zone came certain influences significant for the constitutional history of the towns. Episcopal rule in a town was a phenomenon common to all Europe in the high middle ages and was an inheritance from the late Empire; the decisive stimuli which brought about the transformation of the personal bond uniting the merchant gild members, the export traders who held political power in northwest Europe, into a communal government with a territorial and corporative organization, came from the urban communities of the south, which had from the beginning been familiar with law covering an urban territory. In my opinion the area of association between Romans and Germans, especially in the region of the Meuse, produced institutional contacts pregnant with consequences. Following the example of southern Europe, here for the first time in the north the town was conceived as an enfranchised territory. The legal maxim "Town air makes one free" (*Stadtluft macht frei*) came from Spain and Italy. This does not preclude the existence of seeds favoring the development of this principle, especially in community associations of the Frankish type, which, affected by breezes from the south, grew to maturity and at last flowered.

The institution of town government by consuls spread out from Italy; in some cases the participation of the nobility in urban government can be seen even in the towns of the north, and sometimes the nobles there built towers which served them as residences. It is less common to find the institution of a *podestà* [chief magistrate] in the towns north of the Alps, although the south of France, and, to a certain degree, Regensburg, followed the Italian example in this respect. The towns of northwest Europe, in fact, were limited to their own special form of rule by a mayor or burgomaster.

In reality the constitution of the medieval town everywhere owed its truly original cast to the irresistible forces proceeding from association — more particularly from the association bound by oath, which is a phenomenon common to all Europe. Such association was to a large degree Germanic, although indeed not all these associations were of Germanic origin and although they also show distinct differences as one moves from north to south. In the Italian *conjuratio* [sworn association] the preliminary step of the gild was lacking. From the merchant gild and its idea of society, as the statutes of the gild of Saint-Omer, for example, reveal in such life-like terms, came that powerful outpouring of human brotherhood which actuated the Frankish sworn associations and does not appear in the statutes of Italian towns.

The medieval town, characterized economically by the fundamental role played in its development by commerce and manufacture, and institutionally by the outstandingly associative quality of its entire public life, for the first time in history conferred upon economic man his full political rights. In this respect, a point of unity to be found among different types, the towns of the middle ages stand out from the aristocratic urban culture of the preceding classical towns, which were primarily political, military and cultural centers.

The elements of town life which were typical of the middle ages are naturally found in their purest form in the towns of northwest Europe. The type which these towns represent was, moreover, the most widespread; it appears in Germany beyond the Elbe, in Poland, in Bohemia, in Moravia, and in northern Hungary. The towns of southern Hungary as well as those of Russia belong to another urban type, which is extra-European. In the comparison of the towns of the German heartland and of colonial Germany, one can see that the contrast made in the past between a town which developed organically and a town created as a whole still retains a large part of its value. All the same, it has lost some of its pertinence, for if the residence of the lord and the merchant colony were elements created *ex nihilo,* they became towns in the full sense of the word only at the end of a long process of organic evolution.

At all times and in all countries, the lord — be he king or noble — who founds towns or who, by a legal act, raises rural localities to the dignity of towns, has given birth to urban groups presenting a special type. Towns lent themselves admirably to becoming points of crystallization in a territorial state with established institutions, for they were at the same time concentrations of population, fortified settlements and administrative centers. Thanks to the legal principle that "town air makes one free" and to the fact that the burghers were subject exclusively to an urban court, the town as a region of legal autonomy was distinguished — to its benefit — from the countryside, where there was a complicated legal situation due to the tangle of seigneurial rights. The creation of an urban center attracted population, assured control of newly-conquered country, sometimes even permitted the conquest of disputed regions. As examples it is sufficient to note the foundation of towns in Spain following the Reconquest, *sauvetés* and *bastides*[4] in

[4] Southern French terms for new towns, meaning etymologically "sanctuaries" and "fortifications." [Editor's note.]

southern France, the *villes neuves* in northeastern France, royal and baronial towns in Germany. These towns, built where nothing stood before, provide excellent materials for the historian who seeks to classify towns into special types, because they can often be sorted into groups or families which present identical legal and topographical characteristics. In Germany, where the nobles were above all builders of castles who only slowly and with some hesitation set to work establishing towns, such urban centers are found principally in the thirteenth or fourteenth centuries. Consequently there are grounds for distinguishing in the urban phenomenon a sort of chronological ranking which is sometimes superimposed on a ranking by region.

These created towns make up an important percentage of small medieval towns. Medieval towns can, naturally, be classified as large, medium and small. What was characteristic of large towns, that is, those of more than 10,000 inhabitants, was that in their economic structure, long-range trade and manufacture for export supported each other. Thus at Nuremburg the metal working industry could attain European fame because the town's trade provided its raw materials. The economic structure of a town affected its social structure, in the sense that it gave birth to a powerful patrician class which possessed the political control of the town. Although this political control was often contested in the course of violent conflicts, the patricians succeeded in keeping themselves in power for a long time in a number of towns. The medium-sized towns had a more limited range of economic action. Their export trade had only a few outlets and their economic importance was based on a regional market and on handicrafts. H. Amman has given small towns, containing less than 2,000 inhabitants, a new description: they were not villages provided with walls and restricted by a sense of rural self-centeredness, but centers which in their import and export trade also participated somewhat in the economic life of the late middle ages.

While the differentiation by major regional types seen at the beginning of urban history and presented at the start of this paper is clearly the most fundamental, the differentiation between large, medium and small towns permits the completion of the distribution map of the towns at the end of the middle ages.

Medieval towns present no uniformity. This is what makes their history so interesting and, at the same time, so difficult. The study of historical urban types and their areas of distribution and penetration permits the discovery of a disconcerting multiplicity of new aspects and leads to a more profound understanding of this fundamental phenomenon of western history.

II. ENGLAND AS A TEST CASE

A Review of the Early Theories

CHARLES PETIT-DUTAILLIS

Charles Petit-Dutaillis (1868–1947) devoted his scholarly life to writing which clarified the comparative history of medieval England and France. After his studies at the École des Chartes, the distinguished Parisian school for training archivists and palaeographers, he taught for some years at the University of Lille, and then in 1908 became rector of the University of Grenoble. From 1916 till his retirement in 1936 he was inspector-general and director of the National Bureau of French Universities and Schools in Foreign Countries. His administrative experience enriched his scholarship, which included works on Louis VIII (who successfully invaded England in 1216) and the French communes and a brilliant comparative book, *The Feudal Monarchy in France and England.* Feeling that the magisterial *Constitutional History of England* by William Stubbs was both improperly ignored by French readers and in need of revision, he encouraged one of his students, Georges Lefebvre, to translate the three volumes, and himself prepared three volumes of correction and commentary, which were later published in English. His chapter "The Origin of the Towns of England" reviews the work of Stubbs and other writers of a distinguished generation of students of English municipal history. Its comments are addressed particularly to a French audience.

FRANCE in the Middle Ages was acquainted with infinitely varied forms of free or privileged towns, and very diverse too are the names which were used to designate them from North to South. In England the degrees of urban enfranchisement are less numerous, — the upper degrees are wanting — and, in addition, a somewhat peculiar term is applied to the privileged town in the later centuries of the Middle Ages: in opposition to the *villa,* to the *township,* it is called *burgus, borough,* and the municipal charters often contain in their first line the characteristic formula: "Quod sit liber burgus." [1] Hence in the works of English scholars who concern themselves with the origin of municipal liberties, the word borough is constantly made use of. It seems to us, necessary, however, to get rid of this word, which uselessly complicates and confuses the problem to be solved, and it is well to give our reasons at the outset.

The first idea that the word *borough* summons up is that of the "bonne ville" as it used to be called in France; that is to say, the town which sent representatives to the assemblies of the three estates. In fact, in the fourteenth and fifteenth centuries, the borough is the town which is represented in the House of Commons. But if we are not content to stop short at this external characteristic, and if we enquire in virtue of what principles a town is selected to be represented in Parliament, we are obliged

[1] Below, p. 83, article 1. [Editor's note.]

From Charles Petit-Dutaillis, *Studies and Notes Supplementary to Stubbs' Constitutional History,* vol. I, translated by W. E. Rhodes (Manchester, 1908), pp. 67–90. Reprinted by permission of Manchester University Press.

to recognise that such principles do not exist, that the list of boroughs is arbitrarily drawn up by the sheriffs, and that it even varies to a certain extent. In the period before the application of the parliamentary system, is the boundary line which separates the boroughs from the simple market towns and villages any clearer?

Already, in his valuable book on the gild merchant, which is so full of ideas, facts and documents, Mr. Gross[2] had observed that the term *liber burgus* is a very vague one, applying to a group of franchises the number of which gradually grew in the course of centuries, and none of which, if we examine carefully the relative position of the *burgi* and the *villae,* was rigorously reserved to the *burgi,* or indispensable to constitute a *burgus.* First among them was judicial independence: the burgesses of the *liber burgus* had not to appear before the courts of the shire and the hundred.[3]

In a quite recent work Miss Mary Bateson expresses the opinion that we have there in fact the characteristic of the borough: it is by its court of justice that the *borough,* detached from the hundred and forming as it were a hundred by itself, is distinguished from the Norman period onwards, from the township and the market town. It may have been originally a township, it may continue to be a manor in the eyes of its lord; it is none the less, from a legal point of view, an entirely special institution, which has its place outside the shire and the hundred. It is not a slow evolution, it is a formal act, which gives it this place apart, and which makes of the word borough a technical term corresponding to a definite legal conception. Undoubtedly there is much truth in this theory. But we cannot decidedly accept it in its entirety. The court of justice did not suffice, any more than the tenure in *burgagium* or the *firma burgi,*[4] to constitute a *borough,* at the period at which men claimed to distinguish clearly between the *boroughs* and the market towns. And, *a fortiori,* this must have been the case during the Norman period. We might be tempted to admit, with Mr. Maitland, that it is the character of a corporation, which is the essential part in the conception of a *borough.* But "incorporation" is a legal notion, for which the facts no doubt prepared the way, but which was not stated in precise form until towards the end of the thirteenth century. For the twelfth and preceding centuries we must give up the attempt to find an exact definition of *burgus.* During the Anglo-Saxon period, and even in the eleventh century, the word *burh* had an extremely general signification. It does not even exclusively denote a town, but is also applied to a fortified house, a manor, a farm surrounded by walls.[5]

It should be observed that the important towns are also designated, for example in *Domesday Book,* by the name of *civitates;*[6] like almost all the words in the language of the Middle Ages, *civitas* and *burgus* have no precise and strict application. The difficulty would be the same, or nearly so, if one attempted to define the French *commune* not in an *a priori* fashion but after comparison of all the passages in which the word is employed. In the same way that there is an advantage in making use of this convenient word to denote our most independent towns, it may be of service to use the word *borough,* when we are studying the English towns of the end of the Middle Ages. But, for the period of origins, which is the only one we have before us at present, it is better not to embarrass ourselves with this expression which by its misleading technical appearance has perhaps greatly contributed to plunge certain English scholars into blind alleys. It will be enough to ask ourselves how the towns were formed which have a court of justice and a market, which have a trading burgess population, which have sooner or later obtained a royal or baronial charter, and

[2] On Gross see below, p. 63. [Editor's note.]
[3] Below, pp. 81–84. [Editor's note.]
[4] On the "farm of the borough" see below, p. 98. [Editor's note.]
[5] See Peterborough, p. 46. [Editor's note.]
[6] Below, pp. 68ff. [Editor's note.]

which, both by a variable body of privileges and by their economic development, have distinguished themselves from the simple agricultural groups; whether they were destined to be called boroughs or market towns matters little.

There is no imperious necessity for formulating the problem any differently from the way it has been formulated for the towns of the Continent, and it is for this reason that we have not entitled this essay: *The Origin of the Boroughs.* The question which directly interests general history is to know how the English towns were formed. It is doubtful whether this problem can ever be solved with absolute certainty, but that is no reason for not approaching it at all.

Domesday Book alone can give a solid point of departure for this study. The relatively abundant sources of the Anglo-Saxon period, laws, charters or chronicles, furnish only a very meagre quota to what we know of the towns before the Conquest. It is fortunate again that the "tempus regis Edwardi"[7] was a matter of interest to the commissioners of King William, that we can project the light emanating from *Domesday* on the later times of Anglo-Saxon rule — obscured though that light may often be.

The most serious gap in our sources may be guessed: we have no information as to the filiation which may exist between certain English towns of the Middle Ages, and the towns founded on the same site by the Roman conquerors. During the period of the Roman domination there were no great towns in England. It is believed that Verulamium (St. Albans, in Hertfordshire) was a *municipium;* only four *coloniae* are known: Colchester, Lincoln, Gloucester and York. London was already the principal commercial centre, but we know almost nothing about it. There was without doubt a fairly large number of little towns; the names of some thirty of them have come down to us. Winchester, Canterbury, Rochester, Dorchester, Exeter, Leicester, etc., existed, and doubtless had a germ of municipal organisation.[8] But, in the first place, we know nothing of this organisation, no important municipal inscription having been preserved.[9] Again, we have no idea what became of the Romano-British towns during the tempest of the invasions. At least the precise knowledge which we possess only relates to the disappearance of certain of them, burnt by the Anglo-Saxons, or else completely abandoned, like that curious Calleva Attrebatum (near the present village of Silchester, in Hampshire), of which it has become possible to say — so much have excavations been facilitated in our day by this rapid and definitive abandonment — that it is the best known archæologically of all the Roman provincial towns.[10] Calleva Attrebatum, after the extinction of the imperial government (about 407), was still inhabited for about a century; a recent discovery has shown that they had again begun to speak and write the Celtic language there; then, at the approach of the Germanic invaders the town was completely evacuated, and has never since been inhabited. Other towns, such as Winchester (Venta Belgarum), appear, on the contrary, to have survived the catastrophes of the sixth century; but we know nothing of their ancient institutions. It is more than probable that they resembled those of the Roman towns of the Continent, and in consequence differed essentially from the municipal franchises of the Middle Ages. Nevertheless Th[omas] Wright and H. C. Coote have asserted the continuity of municipal life in England, the filiation of the urban institutions of the Middle Ages and of the Roman period. We can only repeat what Stubbs says of this same theory which he found again in Pearson's *History of England.* All the analogies on which the Romanists rely are susceptible of a different and much more probable explanation. He might have

[7] Below, p. 67. [Editor's note.]

[8] Below, pp. 42ff. [Editor's note.]

[9] Many inscriptions have been discovered since Petit-Dutaillis wrote this. [Editor's note.]

[10] Below, p. 44. [Editor's note.]

added that most French scholars agree today in rejecting this filiation as far as concerns even the most profoundly and anciently Romanised parts of Gaul where municipal life was most intense. What chance remains of there having been continuity in a country like Great Britain in which the imperial domination was much less solidly established? The humble village, with its tenacious agricultural customs, was able to maintain itself as it was, so it is supposed, in the storm of the Germanic conquest, but not the municipality with its institutions.

Certain towns, however, in the material sense of the word, were able, I repeat, to survive the great catastrophe. In spite of the disdain of the Germans for fortified refuges, the ramparts of the Roman towns and imperial fortresses must have been utilised, doubtless even kept in repair for a certain time by the invaders as well as by the invaded, and certain Anglo-Saxon *burhs* must have been only the continuation or the resurrection of Roman fortified places. Such may have been the case with Winchester, Lincoln, Canterbury. In Gaul, a great number of Roman towns perished during the invasion; others, in spite of terrible misfortunes continued to be inhabited, while losing every vestige of their ancient political institutions; life concentrated itself in some particularly favourable quarter, easy of defence, or, with the materials of the abandoned houses, a square *castrum* was constructed, to which the sadly reduced population confined itself. It is probable that this phenomenon of the preservation of fragments of urban life occurred in Britain as elsewhere, and the Germanists have no serious grounds for denying its possibility. In the material sense of the word, certain English urban groups may have continued the Roman town.

Stubbs, we have seen, does not put this supposition absolutely aside. For the rest, if his study of the Anglo-Saxon town is a little wanting in clearness and vigour, at any rate it avoids thereby the faults of too systematic an exposition, and when he examines the formation of the *burh,* which, in his eyes, is nothing but "a more strictly organised form of the township," [11] he assigns a great share to the most diverse influences, and the wealth and variety of the information which his text and notes furnish has not perhaps been sufficiently noticed or turned to profit. We believe with him that in England, as in France, many of the urban communities grew out of preexistent villages. The rural, agricultural character of the town is particularly remarkable in England during the whole of the Middle Ages. Those who study its history, "have fields and pastures on their hands." [12] Part of the townsmen — doubtless the descendants of the most ancient inhabitants — are husbandmen, the cultivated lands are sometimes found even inside the walls, and whatever may have been said to the contrary there are lands belonging to the community of burgesses.

But the towns must have developed above all "in the places pointed out by nature as suited for trade," [13] whether these places were still uninhabited or whether ancient Roman towns or villages existed there already. It was the interest of the kings and magnates to create markets there, which brought them in good revenues, and to guarantee the security of trade; merchants perhaps founded colonies there, as in Germany and France. The "great monasteries in which the Anglo-Saxon bishops had their sees," were also by their economic importance, by the industrial and commercial needs, which the service of religion gave rise to, by the attraction which celebrated relics exercised, centres of urban concentration and work, and Stubbs notes that in the Anglo-Saxon version of Bede the equivalent given for *urbana loca* is *mynsterstowe.*[14]

[11] Stubbs, *Constitutional History* (5th ed.; Oxford, 1891), Vol. I, p. 99.

[12] Maitland, *Township and Borough* (Cambridge, England, 1890), p. 9.

[13] *Constitutional History,* Vol. I, p. 99.

[14] The inventory of the rents and dues owing to the Abbey of St. Riquier . . . shows us, as early as the year 831, a numerous population of lay artisans grouped in streets according to their

Throughout the West the castles also formed the nuclei of urban groupings; they offered a refuge in case of attack, and it was the lord's interest to have for his neighbours artisans and merchants who could supply him with cheap goods. It must have been the same in England. In any case it is quite clear that at one period every English town took on a military character. We may assume that this transformation which was to complete the constitution of towns clearly distinct from villages, took place in the time of Alfred. Until then the word *burh* denoted not a town, but a fortified house belonging to a king or a magnate. In the eighth century the urban settlements, old or new, with the exception perhaps of those which may have grown up around one of these fortified houses, no longer had or never had any serious defence; so that the Danes, when they invaded eastern England in the ninth century, occupied the towns without resistance. By constructing military works for their own use they completed the lesson they were giving the English. Alfred (871–900) knew how to profit by it and created fortified places; and it is from his time that the word *burh,* instead of only denoting fortified houses, is also employed in the sense of town. We see in the Anglo-Saxon chronicle that the valiant warriors, the *burh-ware,* of Chichester and of London, contributed greatly to the success of the war against the Danes.[15] Edward the Elder, son of Alfred (900–924) continued to found *burhs.*[16] We understand henceforth why the documents tell us of *cnihts* dwelling in the towns, and why the first city gilds are *cnihtengilds.*[17]

Mr. Maitland has thrown a flood of light upon this foundation of military towns, which occupy a special place in the county, bear the same name as the county throughout the greater part of England,[18] and in some cases are planted at its geographical centre. The strategic value of these new towns explains why some of them are so small; it is not commercial prosperity nor density of population that gives the latter the special institutions which distinguish them from villages which are sometimes much larger; it is the fact that they are fortified places.

Mr. Maitland goes further. He seeks to explain by purely military causes the differentiation which took place between the township and what he calls the borough; on a study of *Domesday Book* which is certainly ingenious and suggestive, he bases a hypothesis which has been called the "garrison theory"; and he has been followed by another scholar, Mr. Ballard, who systematizes and exaggerates his theory.

Certain towns described in *Domesday Book,* these two scholars observe, are characterised by tenurial heterogeneity, being composed of houses which belong, some (the majority) to the king, others to this or that Norman lord, lay or ecclesiastic; and these houses before the Conquest belonged, some to the king, others to some thegn or other. Thus at Oxford the *burgenses* and their houses or *haws* appertain in some cases to the king, in others to a prelate (the Archbishop of Canterbury, the Bishops of Winchester, of Lincoln, of Hereford, of Bayeux, of Coutances, the Abbot of Abingdon, etc.), in others again to a Norman lord (the Count of Mortain, the Count of Evreux, Walter Giffard, etc.).[19] *Domesday* affords evidence that this is not a Norman innovation, for it gives us a list of *thegns* of the county of Oxford who, before the Conquest, so held houses in the "borough" of Wallingford. Moreover, the possession of many of these houses was in direct relation with the possession of such and such

trades around that abbey, and in return for lands which are granted to them, furnishing some, tools, others bindings, or clothes or articles of food, etc. This very curious document has, it seems to us, the value of a general explanation, in the history of the monasteries and the monastic towns of the West. [Compare Bury St. Edmunds, below, pp. 78–79. Editor's reference.]

[15] See p. 51. [Editor's note.]

[16] See pp. 51–52. [Editor's note.]

[17] See pp. 61–62 and 64–65. [Editor's note.]

[18] The counties lying to the North of the Thames nearly all bear the name of their county-towns; for example Oxford-shire. . . .

[19] See p. 74. [Editor's note.]

a manor in the rural part of the county; indeed the *Domesday* compiler frequently mentions the manor instead of the lord, and indicates how many houses the manor has in the borough: for example, the manor of Doddington has five *haws* in Canterbury. It is specified that before the Conquest, "tempore regis Edwardi," there were in Canterbury 259 houses thus attached to manors; and the rural estates possessing houses in Canterbury numbered thirteen. Not only houses but burgesses appertained to manors: eighty burgesses of Dunwich appertain to one of the manors of Ely, twenty-four burgesses of Leicester to the manor of Ansty, etc. These statements which puzzle the reader of *Domesday*, become intelligible and coherent, if we suppose that every town characterised by tenurial heterogeneity dated from the period at which the Danish invasion had to be repelled, that it was originally essentially a military post, and that its garrison and the upkeep of its ramparts were the concern of the whole county. We can understand then why, side by side with ordinary houses, there are houses which are appurtenances of rural estates, and why, at Oxford, these houses bear the name of *mansiones murales,* and are burdened with the special charge of maintaining the fortifications of the town.[20] Freemen are in fact subject to the *trinoda necessitas,* the triple duty of repairing bridges, serving in war, and maintaining fortifications; the great rural proprietors who wish to acquit themselves of this last obligation without displacing their men, have a house in the town, furnished with *burgenses,* who when the king gives the order, will put in a state of defence the part of the ramparts the care of which is their charge. Many of the *burgenses,* moreover, are warriors, *cnihts,* and are maintained by the king and the great proprietors of the surrounding countryside: in this way is to be explained the mention in *Domesday* of *burgenses* attached to such and such a rural manor. In short, the primitive "borough" is essentially a fortress kept in a state of defence by the inhabitants of the county.

Later, at the end of the Anglo-Saxon period, the military spirit in the borough became enfeebled, a fact which explains the relative ease of the Norman Conquest and the difficulty which we have in reconstituting the real character of the earliest towns. In addition there grew up on the royal demesne, or upon the estates of powerful men, urban groups which obtained tardily, perhaps subsequently to the Conquest, the privileges which the simple townships did not enjoy. These are the homogeneous "boroughs," which are dependent on a single lord; for example, Steyning, which belongs to the Abbot of Fécamp, and whose burgesses are all the Abbot of Fécamp's men. But the real "borough," the primitive *burgus,* is that which, at the date of *Domesday Book,* is still dependent on numerous lords.

This theory is confronted unfortunately by unsurmountable objections. If the inhabitants of a county ought to "contribute" to the upkeep of the ramparts and of the garrison of a particular "borough," and if it is thus that we must explain the mention of houses and burgesses appurtenant to rural manors, how comes it that *Domesday Book* speaks of houses appurtenant to manors which are not situated in the same county as the "borough" in which these houses stand?[21] Why is it impossible to establish a proportion between the number of burgesses furnished by a manor and the extent of that manor, and how is the fact to be explained that a single manor of the Church of Ely maintains eighty burgesses at Dunwich? Why are there so many manors exempt from the burden of maintenance, why are there only three which have duties towards the town of Chester? Moreover, the peculiarities of *Domesday Book,* which the garrison theory claims to render intelligible, are for the most part capable of a simpler interpretation. Miss Bateson has elucidated the position of the *burgenses* appurtenant to rural manors in

[20] *Ibid.* [Editor's note.]

[21] See map of Oxford, p. 75. [Editor's note.]

a very satisfactory manner. They were evidently non-resident burgesses, country people, who, with a view to gain, bought the freedom of a town, in which they might do a profitable trade. The eighty *burgenses* of Dunwich, appurtenant to a manor of the abbey of Ely, had doubtless bought their title, in order to come and buy the herrings which the monks needed, in that port. The houses appertaining to rural lords might serve as occasional lodgings, storehouses, etc. . . . We may add that comparative history does not allow us to consider the "tenurial heterogeneity" of so many English towns very surprising. Material and political dismemberment is the dominant feature of the French and German towns up to the eleventh century. The town was nothing but a juxtaposition of patchwork, of fragments of great estates. There is no reason for attributing an absolutely original growth to the English towns, and it is, in our view, singularly rash to spin theories on their origin without constantly recalling to mind the conditions under which the towns of the Continent appear to have developed.

We propose then to accept the views of Mr. Maitland on the foundation of numerous fortified places in the time of Alfred and his successors, but to reject his theory, made even less acceptable as systematized by Mr. Ballard, on the alleged distinction, of a purely military character, between the "borough" and the township. The creative element of this distinction was doubtless, in England as on the Continent, commerce. Even at the period of the creation of the military *burhs* the economic factor must have played its part; except in some cases in which strategic considerations stood in the way, the king doubtless chose trading places, which it was all important to defend and convert into defensive centres, for fortification and the development in them of the military spirit: such was evidently the case with London. It is evident, besides, that the transformation of a town into a *burh* must have singularly facilitated the development of its trade, since the king's peace specially protected *burhs.* A good situation on a navigable river or on an old Roman road, and commercial traditions, on the one hand, the special security due to the ramparts, the garrison, the king's peace, on the other hand, may have thus had a reciprocal action. The military occupation of the towns thus completed and did nothing but complete the work accomplished under the powerful stimulus of commercial and industrial needs. And it is significant that, in the Anglo-Saxon laws, we sometimes find the town designated by the name of *port,*[22] and that numerous charters tell us of a town's officer called port-reeve or port-gerefa.[23] The *port* is the place of commerce; it is the old name for a town in Flanders, where civic origins have a clearly economic character.[24]

Thus the Anglo-Saxon towns, like the towns of the Continent, were formed in the places in which the insufficiency of agricultural life made itself felt, where the chance of leading a less laborious, more spacious, even safer life than that of the peasant offered itself. In England, as elsewhere, the monastery and the castle served as nuclei of urban concentration. There as elsewhere the creation of markets attracted colonies of traders, and, thanks to the special protection of the king, the town was an abode of peace, a peace safeguarded by a doubtless rigorous penal code.[25] There as

[22] Notably in a passage in the laws of Athelstan, in which *port* is clearly synonymous with *burh* [p. 54, and note Pirenne, p. 2. Editor's reference.]

[23] [Writ of Edward the Confessor, p. 61. Editor's note.] There is also the *port-moot* or *port-manmoot,* the *port-men,* etc. These words apply to inland towns as well as to seaports. [For instance, Ipswich, p. 65. Editor's note.]

[24] The different causes which favoured the growth of towns can be clearly distinguished in the county of Durham. According to the *Boldon-Book,* this county possessed five towns at the end of the 12th century. The external conditions which had determined their development were: at Durham, the castle and the church; at Norham, the castle; at Wearmouth, the sea-port; at Darlington, the high-road; at Gateshead, the close vicinity, on the other bank of the Tyne, of the town of Newcastle, of which Gateshead was in some sort the suburb. [*Cf.* list, p. 87.]

[25] See the case of Chester, pp. 76–78. [Editor's note.]

elsewhere walls gave the citizens a security unknown to the rustic population. The Anglo-Saxon town, it is true, possesses a special franchise: it is a hundred by itself, it has its *moot,* its court of justice. It owes this point of superiority over the French town to the survival of the Germanic institution of the hundred among the Anglo-Saxons. But, like the towns of the Continent at the same period, it is heterogeneous, split up, and its judicial unity is interfered with by private jurisdictions; *sac* and *soc* correspond to immunity.[26] It has no corporate unity: it has indeed associations, gilds; but these are pious or charitable brotherhoods, clubs whose main business is to brew beer and drink it at the common expense;[27] they are not corporations taking part in the government of the town. Of merchant gilds, whose interest it would be to manage common affairs, there is as yet no trace either in the documents of the Anglo-Saxon period or even in *Domesday;* it has been proved, moreover, that later, when there were merchant gilds, they did not constitute the kernel of municipal administration.[28] And this is another feature common to the towns of England and those of the Continent, that the gild, while it was an element of progress and of joint defence against oppression, was not the creative element of civic self-government.

From what Stubbs says it is evident that we are as badly informed respecting the inner life of the primitive English towns as respecting that of the towns of the Continent. We know nothing which allows us to assert the existence of a true municipal patriciate; there is no proof that the possessors of sac and soc, such as the *lagemen* of Lincoln, had administrative powers.[29] We see clearly what the burdens weighing upon the "burgenses" are: payment of *geld* and dues in kind (*firma unius noctis*[30] and others) to the king, payment of *gafol* to the lord of the manor, military service, etc.; but we do not see what their liberties are. It is true that the description of such liberties was not one of the objects for which the Anglo-Saxon charters and *Domesday Book* were drawn up. It is very probable, moreover, that, as early as the eleventh century, the burgesses, emboldened by wealth and peace, had sought for safeguards against the financial tyranny of the royal officers, had dreamed of independence; they had evidently more cohesion and strength than the inhabitants of the country. They asked to be allowed to pay the sheriff an annual fixed sum, instead of numerous little imposts which made exactions easy; at Northampton the *firma burgi* already exists at the time of *Domesday.*[31] At this period, the movement of revolt against seignorial oppression has already begun in some continental towns. Everywhere the increase of moveable wealth created a powerful class of townsmen, careful to safeguard their material interests and able to enforce their claims.

It would perhaps be allowable to say that from that time forward divergencies show themselves between the towns of England and those of the rest of the West. And yet, while it is true that city-republics analogous to those of Italy or Flanders are not found across the Channel, we must not think that the island was not open to continental influences. The present generation of English scholars has only quite recently set itself to determine these influences, and the results obtained have already changed all received ideas as to the development of the English towns. "Our characteristic belief that every sort of 'liberty' was born of ideas inherently English," writes one of these scholars, "must receive another check, and must once more be modified to meet certain facts that have failed to obtain due recognition." . . .[32]

It was thought until recently that the

[26] See p. 78 and glossary. [Editor's note.]
[27] See pp. 63–64. [Editor's note.]
[28] See pp. 63–66. [Editor's note.]
[29] See p. 78. [Editor's note.]
[30] This is a payment of provisions enough to entertain the king and his retinue for one night. [Editor's note.]
[31] See pp. 98ff. [Editor's note.]
[32] Mary Bateson, "The Laws of Breteuil," *English Historical Review, XV* (1900), p. 73. [Editor's note.]

customs of Bristol had served as a model to a great number of English towns; it was, in most of the cases, a mistake, arising from a faulty translation of the place-name Britolium. Miss Bateson has shown that at least seventeen towns of England, Wales and Ireland, perhaps twenty-five, had been granted the customs and franchises of the little Norman town of Breteuil, that several of these seventeen towns — Hereford, Rhuddlan and Shrewsbury — served in their turn as models to others, had daughter towns, even grand-daughter towns. Thus Breteuil played the same part in England as Lorris or Beaumont-en-Argonne in France, or Freiburg-im-Breisgau in Germany. It was not a very ancient or very celebrated town; it first appears in history about 1060 when Duke William built a castle there; but William Fitz-Osbern, to whom the castle of Breteuil was entrusted, became one of the greatest personages of Norman England, and it is to him and his powerful family that the diffusion of the customs of Breteuil is due. This diffusion took place principally in the March of Wales, and its history shows how, by the creation of castles and of free towns the Norman barons definitively colonised and subjected regions far from the centre of government where the pressure of the royal power was comparatively weak. The castle was generally constructed near an already existing village; the village was converted into a free town, or even in some cases a new town was built beside the village. The creation of a market, the assured custom of the garrison, the bait of the franchises of Breteuil, attracted settlers. The former inhabitants of the village continued to cultivate the land, whilst the new population, endowed with very small holdings, comprising, for example, a house and a garden, gave themselves up to industry and commerce. At times even a third element placed itself side by side with the two others; at Shrewsbury, for instance, there was a colony of French merchants, who lived apart and under a régime which had some special features. The article of the customs of Breteuil to which the burgesses attached the most value was doubtless that which reduced the maximum fine to 12 pence.[33] It is to be found in the customs of many towns of Wales, Ireland, Devon, Cornwall, etc., which did not enjoy the rest of the franchises of Breteuil.

Thus the process of urban colonisation, employed throughout the whole extent of France by the church, the feudal baronage and the crown, employed also to civilize Germany, at first by Charlemagne, then by the emperors and princes of the twelfth and thirteenth centuries, was also applied in England. The "ville neuve" is to be found there with franchises borrowed from a French prototype.

It cannot, however, be denied that the development of the English towns had a somewhat peculiar character, — above all, because it was slower than on the Continent and was incomplete. The English towns never attained complete independence; during the whole of the Middle Ages they remained rather small urban groups. Must we conclude from this that the Anglo-Saxon genius was ill-adapted for city life, and was only at its ease in the organization of the village and the agricultural group? We will not invoke the "genius of the race"; it is better to explain this fact by the economic conditions peculiar to mediæval England and by the extraordinary power of its monarchy.

[33] See Hereford, p. 76, and Rhuddlan, p. 78. [Editor's note.]

Pirenne's Theory Applied to England

CARL STEPHENSON

Carl Stephenson (1886–1954) took his Ph.D. under Charles Homer Haskins and Charles Gross at Harvard in 1914, taught at a number of universities including Wisconsin, and was Professor of History at Cornell University from 1930 until his retirement. In 1924–25 a Commission for Relief in Belgium fellowship took him to Ghent to work with Pirenne, and in 1926 he published his first article applying Pirenne's theory of mercantile settlement to the origin of English towns. In 1930 he published an article elaborating this theme in the *English Historical Review,* and in 1933 the Mediaeval Academy of America published his *Borough and Town,* in which he presented his thesis with greater detail and precision. The following extract is taken from the conclusion of that book.

THE TWELFTH-CENTURY BOROUGH is very familiar. We have no trouble in recognizing it as a town — such a town as was still to be met with in any English county down to the Industrial Revolution. It was, of course smaller and dirtier and more crowded than are most towns of to-day. It was hidden behind walls that have now largely disappeared. It was populated by men who wore strange clothes and carried stranger weapons. But fundamentally it seems to us quite comprehensible, for its life was predominantly mercantile. Its shops and warehouses, its markets and wharves, its homes of traders and artisans, spread below an occasional church tower or feudal battlement, constituted a picture that we know, and know intimately.

It is true that the town-dwelling class was then much more sharply distinguished from the rural classes than is the case at present, but that fact does not prevent our feeling well acquainted with the burgess. Indeed, it is easier for us to understand his position in the world than to understand that of the villein, or even that of the baron, — so bourgeois is our modern society. We do not have to be told what is implied by free urban status. It is rather feudal than burgage tenure that has to be explained to us. We sympathize with the burgess in his insistence on what to us seem ordinary rights, and in his demand for a court to enforce them. We readily perceive why townsmen objected to seignorial exploitation and were willing to pay well for the chance to manage their own affairs.

The difficult problem for the student of mediaeval life, accordingly, has never been to describe the borough in the twelfth century, but rather to account for its sudden prominence. Thenceforth the town attained a constantly mounting importance in state and society. Why had it earlier been so obscure?

Since the majority of boroughs had long occupied well recognized positions on the map, it was at first asserted that the mediaeval towns, in all fundamental respects, were merely surviving Roman cities or newer foundations made in imitation of them. But this theory, when attacked by historians of the Germanist school, was shown to be based on little besides sheer assumption. It followed, therefore, that the borough was essentially a mediaeval product; that it somehow arose or was made in the period following the barbarian invasion

From Carl Stephenson, *Borough and Town* (Cambridge, Mass., 1933), pp. 205–213. Reprinted by permission of the Mediaeval Academy of America.

of Britain. And the Germanist explanation hardly advanced beyond such a vague generalization; for every attempt to frame a simpler and more definite formula ended in confusion. To derive the twelfth-century borough from the borough-building activities of Dane and Saxon in the tenth century, despite all continuity of name, proved impossible. When one set of boroughs had been reasonably accounted for, it only became more apparent that another had not been. So Maitland's vivid picture of the old military borough left the mercantile borough an unsolved mystery. So Mary Bateson, by demonstrating the revolutionary nature of the new borough, made its connection with the original borough more obscure than ever.

Meanwhile, on the Continent, similar sources had led to similar speculation, which had ended in a similar *impasse*. But eventually the difficulty was avoided by refusing to take for granted that an older structure, whether called *civitas, urbs, burgus,* or anything else, was originally more than it was proved to be by contemporary evidence. The same procedure must be followed in dealing with the English towns. However natural it may be to regard the twelfth-century borough as a mere continuation of the earlier institution that bore the same name, such a presupposition is unwarranted and misleading. The primitive borough must be studied quite apart from all associations made familiar by later usage.

This approach to the subject inevitably leads to the acceptance of Maitland's central thesis. The older sources clearly depict a borough the essential importance of which was military. Some boroughs were Roman fortifications adapted to the needs of combatants in the ninth and tenth centuries; others were new constructions. Many boroughs, particularly of the latter sort, were short-lived; but many, becoming identified with the freshly organized kingdom of England, continued as permanent centres of administration. And it would seem that the models for these official boroughs were those of the old Roman cities which, because of their strength, had continued to be used by the Saxon conquerors for royal residences, courts, mints, and markets. But whatever the precise origin of such administrative arrangements, it is they which appear to have dominated the tenth-century borough, not mercantile activity.

Contemporary trade was virtually restricted to the petty exchange that served to multiply local markets throughout the Dark Age; the most important transactions were in slaves[1] and live stock.[2] The commerce that reached an English port from overseas was as yet too slight to differentiate the mass of its inhabitants from the population of the countryside. As late as the reign of Edward Confessor we find almost no indication of a socially distinct burgess class. On the contrary, the *burhwaru* of the older type are revealed by the records to have been predominantly agrarian. The outstanding borough-dweller was the *cniht* — a man of thegnly or semi-thegnly rank, an aristocrat who rode and fought, and who gained a living from lands tilled by poorer dependents. If he had a house within the walls, the location was dictated rather by gentlemanly preference than by business opportunity. If a peasant came to reside there, he remained a peasant. As yet there was no common borough privilege, no uniform burgage tenure, no characteristic burgess law. Judicially and fiscally *burhwaru* were still included under a territorial system devised for the country at large. Such a borough lacked all the conspicuous features of urban life.

Finding the original borough so widely and so profoundly different from the twelfth-century borough, we are constrained to suppose a transitional period when one was produced from the other. At what time, under what impetus, and by what process was the change effected? To formulate definite answers to all these questions is extremely difficult, perhaps impos-

[1] See p. 87. [Editor's note.]
[2] See the transactions envisaged in the laws, pp. 54–55. [Editor's note.]

sible. Nevertheless, we are not without positive information on which to base a few intelligible conclusions.

That the later borough was fundamentally mercantile is beyond doubt. Commerce underlay its social structure, and on this, in turn, was built its legal and political constitution. To analyze the municipal charters is to be convinced that the boroughs to which they were granted were essentially trading communities. The typical burgess appears as a trader. His liberties, adapted to his own particular calling, serve to distinguish him from members of the military and agrarian classes. And when self-government emerges in the borough, it is so intimately associated with the bourgeois status of the new age, and so completely unknown in rural communities, that we are led to accept it as a peculiarly urban development.

A borough of this sort could arise only in an age that had become extensively commercial. Such a complex institution could not be wrought by king or by army; it could not be created by official pronouncement. Nor could it grow from a mere cattle market. The development of urban life required commerce on a larger scale — on a European scale. That is why it is impossible to dissociate the history of English towns from the history of Continental towns. If in France and Germany trade was insufficient to permit extensive urban life before the later eleventh century, we should not expect flourishing towns in Britain during the ninth and tenth centuries. The burden of proof assuredly lies with those who assert that the early borough was more than a fortress and an administrative centre.

It is in this connection that Domesday Book is of inestimable value for the study of the towns. The great survey shows that the salient features of the old borough in 1066 were still military and agrarian. Exceptions there were, but the facts which Domesday emphasizes and reiterates on page after page are such as positively deny the existence of the twelfth-century urban system. We are thus given no choice but to decide that in general the system was the product of the Norman period — whether through conscious reform on the part of the conquerors or through the effect of revolutionary forces stimulated by their conquest.

Neither factor can be ignored. The deliberate establishment by Norman barons of new boroughs after French models is incontestable. And the same policy was followed by William himself. At Norwich, Nottingham, and Northampton it must have been he, rather than subordinates, who founded the French boroughs. In such localities as these the new settlers are portrayed as the recipients of special privilege — the same kind of privilege that eventually came to characterize towns in all regions. At Hereford in 1086 this privilege was still restricted to the French colony;[3] later it came to be shared by the whole borough. The twelfth-century custom of Shrewsbury seems to have been produced in the same way. Moreover, there is excellent reason to suppose that a similar development took place at Nottingham; for the testimony of Domesday, together with the results of topographical study, leads us to believe that there also a new régime began in 1066. Individually, the obscure references of the survey to French colonists in other boroughs prove little, but their cumulative effect is very considerable. If the establishment of 125 French traders at Norwich could lead to such tremendous results for the history of the town, what was the effect of the 145 who are reported at York? And while these changes were being effected in lesser boroughs, what was happening at London? For every newcomer in any other single borough there must have been a dozen in the capital. Was their influence proportionately as great as it was at Hereford?

Altogether, the presumption is strong that in most old boroughs the establishment of uniform privilege came only under the Normans. The principal cause, we may well believe, was the insistence upon such

[3] See p. 76. [Editor's note.]

guarantees by the mercantile class; but another fact powerfully contributed to the same result. Down to the Norman Conquest the borough remained the centre of political life in England. Saxon aristocrats not only owned land in the borough; they often lived there as well. We shall probably not be wrong in imagining the population of the old borough largely made up of an official, military class, together with its dependents. But this situation was revolutionized by the Norman conqueror. After 1066 it was the castle which, as a fortress and as administrative headquarters for the royal government, dominated the countryside. The feudal nobility did not live in boroughs, and these, consequently, were allowed to become exclusively bourgeois.

The change was not effected all at once. Years were spent in the erection of the new fortifications, the establishment of new tenants, and the organization of the new governmental system. Many ancient arrangements were left to die a natural death together with the men who had upheld them. As late as 1086 Domesday describes the boroughs as still being essentially what they were under Edward the Confessor. And yet, by the time of Henry I, the old order has disappeared; the borough stands with its new social constitution complete. Very likely we should attribute much to the energy and ability of that great king — notably the fixing of the *auxilia burgorum*[4] and the perfection of the Cinque Ports confederacy. But more of the change must have come as the culmination of a slow process. With the opening of the twelfth century, the older generation of men who had survived the Conquest was gone; and with it vanished the remnants of many an ancient and honorable institution. . . .

These conclusions are not intended to imply that the urban life of early England was exclusively or necessarily a Norman product. According to the view here advanced, it hardly mattered whether a given community was French or English, Danish or Irish. Such questions as who erected the fortifications, who owned the soil, or who ruled the district, can be generally ignored in accounting for the rise of a town. The burgage tenure of the twelfth century, by whatever name it was called, was more than a foreign importation. Its substance would probably have been the same if there had been no Norman Conquest. London's charter[5] might well have contained the same major articles if it had been granted by a son of Harold, rather than by a son of William. We have every reason to suppose that many boroughs would have developed a mercantile population and secured uniform privilege under any dynasty. For the commercial revival that was sweeping Europe would have reached Britain in spite of all variations in its political history. Old cities were there destined to regain their prosperity and new settlements to appear as rivals, whether or not they received the laws of Breteuil.

Indeed, a beginning in this direction was already evident in England before 1066. We may doubt the organization of the Cinque Ports under Edward Confessor, but not the foundation of the Dover liberties. Scandinavian trade had brought considerable population to York, Lincoln, and Norwich; and London must have been greater than any of them. Droitwich seems to have grown from saltworks in Saxon times, and Dunwich from herring fisheries. Some municipal privilege had certainly emerged in a few progressive localities, and may have existed in others concerning which we have no information. But as yet it was exceptional and restricted. It had not come to characterize the ordinary borough.

Thus it was left for the Norman Conquest to continue a process which had barely started when William landed at Pevensey. The perfection of urban organization was impossible without the establishment of a new social grouping. This the invaders, though not entirely conscious of what they were about, accomplished with revolutionary speed and thoroughness.

[4] See p. 98. [Editor's note.]

[5] See p. 80. [Editor's note.]

Results that might have demanded a century of slow development were achieved inside the lifetime of one generation. In an age when reviving commerce was just gaining headway on the continent, England was brought into close union with a Continental state, and all traditional institutions that might have hampered the complete triumph of the mercantile class in the boroughs were swept aside. The consequence was the sudden appearance in the twelfth century of a uniform urban system that Saxon England had never known. And if any one hesitates to believe that the span of a half-century was sufficient for so great a transition, he has only to remember how the same period affected other phases of English civilization. In the constitutional, ecclesiastical, military, and cultural history of the nation the Norman Conquest began a new era. To accept that event as crucial also for the development of the towns is merely to follow the results of long established criticism.

The Anglo-Saxon Origins of the English Borough

JAMES TAIT

James Tait (1863–1944) was educated at Manchester and Oxford, returned to Manchester to teach at the age of 24, and became Professor of Ancient and Medieval History in the University of Manchester in 1902. In 1919 he retired from teaching in order to devote himself to writing a definitive history of the English borough. For this work he was unusually well prepared by the great variety and precision of his scholarship. For 10 years he had written biographies for the *Dictionary of National Biography*. His reviews of many books on different subjects were models of balanced criticism and appreciation; the one he wrote of Maitland's *Domesday Book and Beyond* found the crucial weaknesses in that book and earned Maitland's gratitude. And in the years of his prime he contributed extensively to the *Victoria County History*, edited chronicles, charters and a section of Domesday Book, wrote on place-names, and produced a thoughtful and original book, *Medieval Manchester*.

The selection reprinted below is taken from *The Medieval English Borough* which Tait published in 1936. This volume is solidly based on detailed and critical scholarship; it reveals an author who disliked showmanship, overstatement and speculation and who preferred to criticize the syntheses and explanations of others rather than to offer alternatives of his own. The following extract, intended as a summary and general conclusion of his work on the Anglo-Saxon period, is in large part simply a recasting of the review he wrote of Stephenson's *Borough and Town*.

If the foregoing reconsideration of the evidence leaves no room for the old idea, which was still held by Miss Bateson, that a specially created urban court formed a universal legal criterion of the early borough, it does not bear out Dr. Stephenson's contention that his own criterion of mercantile settlement was generally absent, and the normal borough merely an agricultural group much of the usual manorial type. Every borough had a market and every borough was a *port*, a

From James Tait, *The Medieval English Borough* (Manchester, 1936), pp. 130–138. Reprinted by permission of Manchester University Press.

place of trade. The early trade even of the more considerable of these ports must not be judged by the standard of the great cities of the Netherlands, which, with rare exceptions, they never reached. Yet by the end of the Anglo-Saxon period, many of them were evidently prosperous. Of the thirty-five for which Domesday gives statistics of population in 1066, twenty-one had more than 200 burgesses and five of these (not including unsurveyed London and Winchester) more than 900, involving total burgess populations of from about 1000 to about 9500.[1] In a large proportion of these cases we should feel sure that the burgesses had some other means of support than agriculture, even if Domesday did not tell us that the 1320 burgesses of Norwich had only 180 acres of arable and the 538 of Ipswich (which had eight parish churches) only forty, and that among the vast majority of the burgesses of Colchester the average share of the individual was only a little more than a quarter of the villein's yardland.

In his article of 1930 Dr. Stephenson recognized no real towns outside the seaports of the south-east, but since then he has been impressed by some of the population figures and in his book *Borough and Town,* admits a considerably wider extension of urban trade. In his concluding chapter the large populations of York, Lincoln and Norwich — he might also have added Thetford with its 943 burgesses [in 1066] — are recognized as evidence of Scandinavian trade. The fisheries of Dunwich and the salt industry of Droitwich are noted. He is even ready to allow that the beginnings of municipal privilege may have extended beyond the south-eastern seaports, though evidence of this is wanting, and that the Norman Conquest only speeded up a process which was well under weigh. But he still maintains that it had not touched the ordinary borough and the line between the ordinary and the extraordinary is left exceedingly vague. The Irish-Scandinavian trade in furs at Chester[2] is obscurely alluded to elsewhere, but nothing is said of the journeys of their cloth merchants as far as Cambridge, of the iron industry of Gloucester, of the presence of *mercatores advenae* [foreign merchants] at Exeter in 1068. The well-attested activity of Anglo-Saxon merchants from Iceland in the north to Rome in the south, the export of English cheese to Flanders, the testimony of William of Poitiers to the skill of their artificers in metal, are not taken into account. Even where mercantile settlement is finally admitted, some inconsistency with earlier arguments is occasionally observable. Not far short of half the population of English Norwich in 1086, for instance, is classed as dependent cultivators and the municipal growth of the city is derived entirely from the settlement of 125 French burgesses in a new borough, the later Mancroft ward, under William I. In this, as in two or three other such new foundations, as at Nottingham and Northampton, there is a certain likeness to the *poorts* of the Netherlands which grew up outside feudal *burgs,* but at Norwich at least the old borough was of a type very different from the *burg* of that region and it is significant that its French neighbour was known as Newport. Dr. Stephenson is inclined to claim cispontine Cambridge as another of these French boroughs, reviving the old theory, combated by Maitland, which packed 400 houses into 28 acres north of the bridge. Not the least of the objections is the apparent continuity of the royal tenement rents from 1066 to 1483.

To such foreign mercantile settlements, Scandinavian in this case, Dr. Stephenson would ascribe even the limited urban development which he now allows to the great Danelaw boroughs at an earlier date. Little or no allowance is made for a like native development in the English boroughs, because he has convinced himself that they were predominantly agricultural. This under-estimate of English trade and urban growth results partly from failure to distinguish always between what Domesday reports for 1066 and what for 1086,

[1] Below, pp. 68ff. [Editor's note.]
[2] See p. 77. [Editor's note.]

and partly from a tendency to interpret ambiguous evidence in the light of a theory. The villeins and bordars and minute or poor burgesses mentioned in a few boroughs were either on *enclaves* of royal or private arable or, in the great majority of cases, obvious victims of Norman devastation, a depressed class of former full burgesses. The 480 *bordarii* at Norwich in 1086 were reduced to the status of "cottagers" because they were unable to pay any customs, *i.e.,* dues, with the burgesses, but it is most unlikely that they had anything but the name in common with the rural bordars. They probably got a precarious living in minor urban occupations. The misunderstanding is the more unfortunate because it is used to support a theory that the mass of the Anglo-Saxon *burgenses* — a term meaning, it is held, no more than "borough people" and covering various classes — were mere cultivators of borough arable which was in the hands of a few rich men. This theory seems to have been suggested mainly by the division of the arable land at Derby and Nottingham between a small number of burgesses. But the arrangement may be more probably explained by a system of leases, such as obtained at Huntingdon, and not as a manorial relation. It may even mean that the "agricultural shell" of the borough was becoming unimportant for the mass of the burgesses. In accordance with his view Dr. Stephenson sees only a small number of individual landowners in the passage: "Burgenses Exonie urbis habent extra civitatem terram xii carucarum." [3] This is grammatically possible, but it is equally possible and more probable that the borough fields of Exeter were divided, as they certainly were at Colchester, between, at any rate, a considerable proportion of the burgess body.

The small borough, especially in the south-west, has a deceptively agricultural look in Domesday. It was often seated in the *caput* of a large royal manor and the revenue from market and burgess rents was included with that of the manor in a single farm. The compilers of the survey were, therefore, not always careful to enumerate the burgesses separately from the villeins and bordars, but the limitation of the earl's third to the borough revenue shows that borough and manor were distinct entities. Where burgesses were few, the borough might sooner or later disappear, as it did for instance, at Bruton in Somerset. On the other hand, a more favourable position for trade already marked out Ilchester, with its 108 burgesses in 1086, for municipal growth. The same variety of fortune befell the similar little groups of burgesses round markets which Norman lords established at their manorial centres after the Conquest. In Hertfordshire, Ashwell and Stansted failed to maintain the urban character which St. Albans retained and extended. Even the smallest Anglo-Saxon boroughs were not essentially different from "mercantile settlements" like these.

In the agricultural borough pictured by Dr. Stephenson, the burgage tenure of the twelfth century could not exist. It came, he holds, with mercantile settlement. Yet we find the essential features of the tenure already present. The tenement is heritable at a money rent, the landgable or "custom of burgesses"; subject to some varying restrictions, it may be sold or mortgaged. Inability to render any custom or exemption from custom excludes from the class of burgesses. Villeins and bordars are usually carefully distinguished from them. Their rents formed a leading item in the fixed farm of the borough, and in 1086 they were complaining that they were held responsible for rents and taxes withheld by Normans who had dispossessed burgesses. The burgage rents were still called landgable. Identities of amount can be proved, as at Cambridge. The rateable area at Oxford was known both before and after the Conquest as the king's "Eight Virgates."

Had the borough been primarily agricultural, the unit of assessment would have

[3] Stephenson translated this as saying that the burgesses of Exeter "have outside the city 12 *carucates,*" i.e., plowlands. [Editor's note.]

been acres in the arable fields; actually it was the house (*domus*) within the ramparts and many burgesses had no share in the fields. As a source of revenue burgess and house were convertible terms. It is true that otherwise land tenure in the boroughs differed little, if at all, from free tenure outside them, but the peculiarities of the later burgage tenure, especially that of devise of land, were not due to foreign innovation but to changes in the common law from which they were protected by their charters. Just as borough law was merely an evolution from general law, burgage tenure of land in England cannot historically be dissociated from the common freehold tenure which came to be known as "socage." As late as 1306 the mayor and aldermen of London reported to the king that all tenements in the city were held *in socagio,* and it was half a century before *in libero burgagio* replaced it in the conservative city.

For long after the Conquest *liberum burgagium* comprised not merely land tenure, but the whole body of burghal privilege, the status of a borough. Thus Henry I granted it to Beverley "secundum liberas leges et consuetudines burgensium de Eboraco."[4] It is not possible to take these "laws and customs" as wholly of Norman introduction. The Domesday surveyors would hardly have devoted a column and a half to the *leges* of Chester before the Conquest, had they become altogether obsolete.[5] Henry I's survey of Winchester shows no radical change there nearly sixty years after that event. The rather irregular landgable rents of 1066 were still in force, and even a few of those occasional personal services which were required from royal burgesses in some Anglo-Saxon boroughs and which Dr. Stephenson regards as inconsistent with real burgage tenure. None of them, however, were servile according to English ideas and they occasionally lingered on to the eve of the thirteenth century. That Norman castle-building and mere ravaging made gaps in certain boroughs, which entailed some early changes, is not to be denied, but they were changes of detail not of principle. The Winchester burgesses of *c.* 1110 seem to have thought that the chief result was too often to substitute *pauperes* for *boni cives.* They certainly did not regard themselves as better off than their Anglo-Saxon predecessors.

York, indeed, and perhaps Winchester, Dr. Stephenson allows to be an exception to his general idea of the Anglo-Saxon boroughs. But a re-examination of the Domesday evidence for the "ordinary" borough of that date points to a substantial continuity with later conditions which the small and lifeless *burg* of the Netherlands, with which he compares it, never exhibited. If absorbed in the *poort,* which did not always happen, the *burg* became a mere fraction of an entirely new organism. In England, on the contrary, the beginnings of urban life were worked out within the walls of its *burhs,* not without them. The universal features were a market and a free burgess tenement of urban type, held at a low rent and within certain limits, which were enforced also after the Conquest, transferable. A purely urban court was less general. The London *husting* was then exceptional and, at the other end of the scale, the minuter of the boroughs of the south-west could have had no other court than those of the hundreds in which they lay. It may, indeed, be conceded to Dr. Stephenson that the court of most boroughs was in origin an ordinary hundred court and that the hundred did not always, as it did at Sandwich, for instance, coincide exactly with the urban area. But the addition of three or four rural vills to such an area, to make up a full taxative hundred or half-hundred, left the court predominantly urban. The needs of traders involved specialization and the tract *Episcopus,* written before 1050, distinguishes between *burhriht* and *landriht.*[6] The appendant vills, the "liberties" of the later municipal boroughs, were a wholly secondary

[4] "According to the laws and customs of the burgesses of York." [Editor's note.]
[5] See pp. 76–78. [Editor's note.]

[6] That is, between borough law and that of the countryside. [Editor's note.]

element in their judicial as in their administrative organization. No argument against the urban character of the pre-Conquest borough can fairly be drawn from the antecedents of a court which persisted into the age of self-government, not infrequently, as at Colchester, under its original name.

In these urban courts, which were administrative as well as judicial, and in their ultimate responsibility for the borough farms, the burgesses could not fail to develop some communal spirit. Its scope was limited, no doubt, before, as for long after, the Conquest by the presidency of a reeve appointed by the king, but it is not unlikely that trading interests were already stimulating communal feeling outside the courts. It may well be that Gross drew too sharp a line between the Anglo-Saxon cnihtengilds of London, Canterbury and Winchester, and the Anglo-Norman merchant gilds.[7] The London cnihtengild continued for half a century after the Conquest to be composed of the leading English merchants and the chapmangild of Canterbury, whose members were *cnihts,* though first mentioned by that name about 1100, has every appearance of a pre-Conquest origin. It was probably indeed, the gild of burgesses which appears in Domesday. Its head significantly was the portreeve of the city, and from his name possibly an Englishman. Dover, too, had its English *gihalla burgensium.* Such gilds are not, indeed, attested elsewhere, but, except at London, they are only casually mentioned and even the later merchant gilds are found only in a minority of boroughs.

The active element in the medieval borough court was naturally its wealthiest and most experienced members. A casual record reveals the existence of this practical aristocracy nearly fifty years before the Conquest in a group of boroughs far remote from the Channel ports. When a bishop of Crediton in 1018 wished to secure full publicity for a mortgage of part of his lands, he sent a formal intimation of it to the witan (*burhwiton*) not merely of the county town, but also of the three smaller boroughs of Devon.[8] This was clearly a recognition of the boroughs as communities, for otherwise he would have sent his notice to the king's reeves of the respective boroughs.

That the Norman Conquest ultimately gave a great impulse to English trade and urban development is not in dispute. The questions at issue are how far it made a new start in this development, and whether the old English borough-port from the first did not contain a germ of urban growth which might indeed come to little or perish, as it did in not a few small "free boroughs" of post-Conquest creation, but which marks it as essentially different from the *burg* of the Low Countries. On this latter point Dr. Stephenson adheres to the view he expressed in his article of 1930. On the first he has yielded a good deal of ground. He no longer maintains that there was no urban continuity between the Anglo-Saxon borough and the Anglo-Norman "town," except in a few seaports of the south-east. But he regards this urban growth before 1066 as quite recent, and he still leaves us with a large and indefinite class of "ordinary" boroughs, agricultural, save for insignificant local trade. Unfortunately, some of the evidence he adduces for this is equally applicable to larger boroughs in which he now admits trading settlement. This seems to be due to insufficient reconsideration of certain conclusions from Domesday in his original article. His study of the Anglo-Saxon borough began with the survey of 1086, and he was too much impressed by features which seemed capable of a non-urban interpretation.

It would be idle to deny that the Anglo-Saxon borough, even in the middle of the eleventh century, had features which were not in harmony with autonomous municipal organization: ecclesiastical and lay immunities, the sokes of the larger towns, burgesses dependent on rural estates, differences of rank, in some cases personal services in addition to money rents. Munic-

[7] See p. 63. [Editor's note.]

[8] See p. 61. [Editor's note.]

ipal autonomy, however, lay in a somewhat distant future. The Norman kings took over the boroughs from their predecessors, subject to rights, partly flowing from land ownership, partly from sovereignty, yielding, relatively to area, a larger revenue than their rural domains. If in some respects the borough system before long became a little more orderly, thanks partly to the influence of the new Norman foundations, in others the disorder was retained and even extended. Feudalism increased the number of sokes and preserved the Anglo-Saxon heriot[9] in some boroughs as a feudal relief. At Norwich, Northampton, and Nottingham, English and French boroughs, with different customs, lived uneasily side by side. The gild merchant while preparing the way for the communal movement and incorporation, which ultimately swept away the relics of a disorderly past, introduced a further conflict of ideas and occasionally severe friction in practice.

[9] Return of a dead man's weapons or other goods to his lord; see Hereford, p. 76. [Editor's note.]

If it is not possible to draw a perfectly sharp line of demarcation in the development of the borough at the Norman Conquest, it is equally difficult to draw such a line at the settlement of the Danes in the northern boroughs or indeed at any earlier date after the permanent reoccupation of the old Roman towns. It is all one story. A study of its various phases certainly discourages the old quest of a neat legal definition of the borough, applicable at all periods. Government officials in the fourteenth century found this no easier than does the student of the Burghal Hidage and Domesday Book. Yet, if, with Dr. Stephenson, it is preferred to find the common thread in the gradual development of a trading community, why should its humble beginnings be ignored?

Levitsky's Artisanal Theory in England

EUGENIA V. GUTNOVA

Yakov Levitsky, a professor of history and senior research associate at the Institute of History of the Academy of Sciences of the U.S.S.R., has specialized in the history of England. In 1954 he and his former teacher at Moscow State University, the late academician E. A. Kosminsky, collaborated on a two-volume work in Russian, *The English Bourgeois Revolution of the Seventeenth Century.* In 1960, he published a book, also in Russian, *Towns and Urban Handicraft in England in the Tenth to Twelfth Centuries,* which has gone almost completely unnoticed in Western Europe and America. A summary of his argument which preserves the outlook and flavor of the book is given by the review published by Eugenia Gutnova in the Soviet journal of medieval history, *Srednie Veka.* Professor Gutnova, also a student of Kosminsky, teaches at Moscow State University and is the author of many studies on medieval England, including a book, in Russian, *The Origin of the English Parliament.*

The monograph by Y. A. Levitsky entitled *Towns and Urban Handicraft in England in the Tenth to Twelfth Centuries* covers the early period of the English towns of the middle ages (mainly tenth to twelfth centuries, with extensive excursions into an even earlier period, the seventh to ninth centuries). The subject

From Eugenia V. Gutnova, *Srednie Veka,* vol. XX (1961), pp. 240–246. Reprinted by permission of Professor Gutnova. I owe the translation to Professor Ivan L. Rudnytsky.

chosen by the author is of significant interest for the history of English medieval towns and also for the broader problem of the appearance of towns in medieval Europe. This subject has not been sufficiently investigated. In Soviet medieval studies, up to the present, there has been no specialized and thorough study of the history of the English towns of this era. On the other hand, in bourgeois and in particular in English historiography this subject has always been seen predominantly from politico-juridical points of view. In the general works and monographs of past and contemporary bourgeois students concerned with the problems of medieval English towns, the attention is focused mainly on the town's political life, the organization into legal classes, and on town laws, customs and privileges, while the social organization of the town and its specific economic nature as compared with the village have remained unilluminated. The questions of the economy of the town are touched upon only in connection with its agrarian structure or, at best, with its commercial activities. This applies in particular to the appearance of towns in England, which is usually explained by bourgeois students by the "burg" or "market" theories and not in connection with the development of the productive forces of English society in the process of feudalization. In contrast to this traditional approach of bourgeois historiography, Levitsky's book represents the first and on the whole a highly successful attempt to study the history of the towns of medieval England from the socio-economic point of view. The author's point of departure on this question is in sharp contrast to the works of all of the bourgeois writers on the subject, for Levitsky begins with the well-known Marxist thesis that medieval towns as centers of production and commerce appeared in the process of the division [of labor] between handicrafts and agriculture,[1] and firmly rejects the arguments of the partisans of the "market" theory (H. Pirenne, R. Sohm, C. Stephenson, *et al.*) that markets and commerce themselves gave birth to the towns. . . .

The book is based on thorough and frequently very subtle analysis of the most variegated sources, and it is literally saturated with the source material, even though the data on the earlier history of medieval English towns are rather widely spread and quite fragmentary (especially for the period before the twelfth century). To reconstruct the picture of the emergence and the early history of English towns, the author was forced to gather his data, grain by grain, from the most diverse sources in which there were dispersed and often indirect references to this subject — from law codes of the Anglo-Saxon era, royal charters, chronicles, various kinds of correspondence, biographies, Domesday Book, Exchequer rolls, etc. The author has used all the material accessible to him and has extracted valuable information from sources of kinds which earlier were not used at all for the study of the history of English towns. One must also note the author's absolute lack of bias in the analysis of the sources. When giving his own interpretation of this or that document, he invariably presents all the other possible interpretations, especially those to be found in the literature, arguing with those with which he disagrees. . . .

The work consists of a short introduction, which gives a critical review of the literature, and five chapters of research. In Chapter I ("The Appearance of Market Centers in England and the Early Stages of Their Development") and Chapter II ("Commerce and Market Centers in England in the Ninth to the First Half of the Eleventh Centuries") the author follows through the sources the development of barter and commerce in England from the middle of the seventh to the beginning of the eleventh centuries and the reflection of this process in law codes, in the evolution of the monetary system and weight units, and in the birth of the system of commercial privileges and custom duties.

In Chapter III ("English Handicrafts

[1] See the quotation from the *Soviet Encyclopedia* in the Conflict of Opinion. [Editor's note.]

about the End of the Tenth Century") the process of the emergence of crafts in England as an independent branch of production, i.e., the process of differentiation of crafts from agriculture, is investigated. This process, as Levitsky convincingly shows, began on a large scale in England only at the end of the tenth, and in the eleventh century, when the first towns began to appear, but the author also fixes its individual symptoms for an even earlier period, the eighth and ninth centuries, showing the course of the gradual division of crafts from agriculture, and their expansion and growth. Chapter IV ("Towns as Centers of Crafts and Commerce in the Eleventh and Twelfth Centuries") examines the economic and social nature of these early towns and this analysis is based mainly on the data about towns given by Domesday Book. Finally, in Chapter V ("Town Crafts and Their Organizations in England in the Twelfth Century") the process of the appearance of gilds in the towns is examined — a problem only slightly considered in the specialized literature. Levitsky shows here the various forms of craft organizations in England and the struggle with the town authorities and the feudal lords of the towns through which the various gilds had to go to defend their right to exist. . . .

One of the most important conclusions presented with broad and convincing arguments in Chapters I and II is the author's thesis that, historically, the appearance of commerce preceded the appearance of towns, i.e., the separation of crafts from agriculture.[1] Levitsky's work clearly shows that in its development commerce passes through a series of stages before it begins to serve the country's growing commodity production, in particular artisanal production, which appears later than the first elements of barter.

During its earliest period of existence (in England in the seventh century), as is clear from Chapter I of this study, commerce had an occasional character — it was mainly external and was conducted by itinerant, most often foreign traders, bringing items of luxury into England and occasionally exporting agricultural products. But already, at the beginning of the eighth century and especially in the ninth century, commerce became a more regular occurrence; it began to include a broader selection of goods appearing on the internal market and in particular the products of the nascent handicrafts. English traders also were beginning to participate. Finally, at the end of the tenth century and in the early eleventh century, a significant expansion of the internal market took place, and the merchants became a settled stratum of the population inside England itself. The number of market centers grew, many of which, as crafts and agriculture gradually separated, turned into towns, i.e., special centers of crafts and commerce.

In this connection we find the particular interpretation which Levitsky offers in Chapter II for the term "port," often encountered in the Anglo-Saxon sources, to be of interest and altogether correct. According to this interpretation, the word "port" in England in the ninth to eleventh centuries meant any marketing center irrespective of whether the latter was a harbor or an inland site. Also, Levitsky's position that straightforward identification of "ports" with towns as centers of craft and commerce is impossible seems correct to us. He shows convincingly that neither the presence of a market in this or that settlement, nor the existence of fortifications (*burh*) or of an administrative center (*civitas*) by itself transformed such a settlement into a town. Such transformation could take place only when an indigenous population of artisans appeared in the "port," i.e., when this marketing place became a center of the newly distinct branch of social production — handicrafts. At the same time, one can only agree with the author also that especially in market places the greatest potential opportunities were created for their transformation into towns, since there existed a relatively broad market for the sale of goods, which was likely to attract the representatives of the newly-forming stratum of specialists, the artisans.

All these observations and conclusions of Chapters I and II of Levitsky's work are not only definitely directed against the "market" theory of the appearance of towns but also reveal the full inconsistency of those bourgeois historical theories (e.g., Dopschianism[1]) which claim the existence of commerce from time immemorial and are inclined to identify its very early and embryonic form with capitalism. . . .

Levitsky's observations in connection with the concrete development of the separation of crafts from agriculture in England of the period under study are of great value, confirming our theoretical considerations on this question. After reading Levitsky's work one can hardly doubt that the transformation of crafts into an independent branch of industry started first of all in the metalworking industry (as early as the eighth century), then in textiles (ninth to tenth centuries), later in the leather trades and other industries (late tenth and early eleventh centuries).

Possibly of the greatest interest are the conclusions of Chapter IV, the central chapter of the work. In it the process of the creation of English towns is captured in all its complexity and dialectical nature. Levitsky's work contributes much which is new to its understanding. The material he introduces leaves no doubt that the appearance of towns in England cannot be of any earlier period than the very end of the tenth or the beginning of the eleventh century and that in Domesday Book the town appears as something still relatively new. The new layer of population (*burgenses*) forming the nucleus of the town population, as Levitsky shows, in many cases was still tightly bound to its agricultural surroundings and to the manors which they left to go to the towns, while still remaining in tenurial and sometimes in personal dependence on their lords.

At the same time, Levitsky convincingly shows that already in Domesday Book the town in its economic constitution was sharply different from a village. It appears, first of all, as a center of artisanal production, which was determining its specific character. The analysis, which the author applies in this connection to the agrarian organization of the early English towns, is of great interest. As is known, the presence in English towns of a system of urban landholding and of communal relations gives many investigators, (e.g., Maitland, Ballard, *et al.*) reason to insist that there were no substantial differences between towns and villages in eleventh-century England. Levitsky's investigation of Domesday Book leaves no doubt that already in this early period the landholdings of town dwellers were so insignificant that these holdings could not assure their existence and may only be considered as a small support to their basic preoccupations of trading and crafts.

One must note the great service the author performs in his critique of the understanding of the term *mercatores* used in bourgeois historiography. This term is arbitrarily translated by the majority of its proponents simply as "merchants." With the facts on hand, Levitsky proves conclusively, as it appears to us, that in the twelfth century, when the division of crafts from commerce was only beginning, the term *mercator* could equally mean a craftsman and a merchant-trader, since as sellers of their own wares craftsmen appear more often than merchants occupied in commerce specifically as "middlemen."[2] This conclusion also definitely hits at the "market" theory and its concomitant points of view, according to which the creators and main inhabitants of the first towns were not artisans but merchants.

Generally the undoubted value of Levitsky's work is in sharp, critical edge directed against bourgeois historiography, which appears not only in the critical re-

[1] Alfons Dopsch (1868–1953), professor of economic and cultural history at the University of Vienna, argued that natural economy and money economy have existed together at all times and in all places, and called the Carolingian economy "early capitalism." [Editor's note.]

[2] [This was also the view of Charles Gross, *The Gild Merchant* (Oxford, 1890), I, 107. — Ed.]

view of the literature of the problem, but also in all of the contents of the work. We already have noted its wide, all-out attack on the "market" theory of the origin of towns and on the most brilliant proponent of this theory in the history of English medieval towns, C. Stephenson. . . . The author also sharply criticizes the much-advertised "garrison" theory of Maitland and his concept of the tenurial heterogeneity of town holdings, which he used in support of his "garrison" theory. On specific topics the author also criticizes the works of J. Tait, C. Gross and other historians. . . . One must note that the criticism of bourgeois theories in the book always relies on specific sources and has quite a concrete and scientific character.

With all these undisputed qualities Levitsky's work is not without certain shortcomings. . . . We have doubts about the author's attempts to consider as items of English export in the eighth and early ninth century the gifts which the representatives of the Anglo-Saxon aristocracy used to send to the continent to their friends and more respected members of the church hierarchy. If such facts are evidence of a certain level of development of craftsmanship (most probably manorial), then they hardly give one a basis for talking about the development of export trade with the manufactured products of craftsmanship.

On the whole this monograph is very valuable, notwithstanding the above remarks. . . . This original, serious work of Levitsky's, filled with solid material, undoubtedly enriches Soviet medieval studies with new findings and conclusions and points up new directions for further research in this area.

III. A SAMPLE OF THE EVIDENCE

Archaeology

Practically all our knowledge of the size, population and manner of life of Roman towns in Britain comes from archaeological research. This evidence cannot be presented here directly, and instead we have a summary of the conclusions of R. G. Collingwood (1889–1943), historian, archaeologist and Professor of Philosophy at Oxford, from the introductory volume of the Oxford History of England. The map is based on the British Government Ordnance Survey, *Map of Roman Britain* (3rd ed., 1956), which marks all Roman settlements known to have had walls. It therefore includes a range of places from the great city of London to small posting-stations, and further excavations may add to the list of small towns. Except for the great *castrum* at Chester, the forts of Roman Britain are not indicated here, although some military camps, like Manchester and the Saxon shore fort of Portchester, became the sites of medieval boroughs.

IT WAS THE AGE of the Antonines that saw the towns of Britain reach their apogee. This was the time when their population was largest, their public buildings most splendid, and their private houses most luxurious. At this point, therefore, we may pause for a moment to survey their achievement and estimate the return they gave for all the effort that had gone to their creation.

We find tribal capitals to the number of a dozen: Canterbury, Chichester, Winchester, Silchester, Cirencester, Dorchester, and Exeter south of the Thames; north of it Leicester, Wroxeter, Caerwent; and Aldborough beyond the Humber. Verulam, too, was in fact a tribal capital, differing from the rest in promotion to municipal rank. These represent the romanized urban life of the Britons. London, the largest of all, and by now almost certainly the seat of government, was perhaps rather cosmopolitan than British, though doubtless its inhabitants were for the most part natives of the province. Bath, too, a luxurious and fashionable health-resort, was a cosmopolitan town that stood outside the tribal system. The colonies of Colchester, Gloucester, Lincoln, and York, in spite of their military origin, were becoming increasingly British as the British element came to preponderate in the army, and were growing less and less different in character from the ordinary run of the larger towns. Smaller towns were numerous. We know about fifty, varying from busy industrial centres to mere posting-stations along the main roads.

In spite of the scale and magnificence of their public buildings, so far in excess of our ordinary modern standards, all these towns, compared with our own, were very small. London contained within its walls 330 acres; Cirencester 240; Verulam 200; Wroxeter 170; Colchester 108; Silchester only 100. Some of the towns which in the preceding paragraph have been classified as large covered no more than 30 or 40 acres. Nor were the inhabitants as a rule at all closely packed within the defences.

ROMAN TOWNS
with modern names

There were no blocks of flats. The houses were detached and stood with plenty of elbow-room. At Silchester, where the entire town-plan has been recovered, at Caerwent, where the plan is hardly less complete, and at Verulam, where trenching has been done with the express purpose of settling the question, it is proved that there were considerable areas towards the outskirts of the town where no houses were ever built. The walls were evidently laid out on a generous scale to make room for large increases of population, and more land was included than was ever required. When we ask ourselves, therefore, what population a town of a given size probably contained, we must be guided by the analogy not of a densely packed modern city with houses touching one another all along its streets, but of a residential town where they stand free.

In Silchester, with 100 acres of land, there were only 80 houses. Half of these are of the humblest kind, inhabited doubtless by a single family with few slaves or none. Even the largest could hardly contain a very large body of slaves in addition to the family. It has been estimated that Silchester might have contained as many as 2,000 inhabitants; as this implies an average of 25 to a house, it ought to be considered extremely generous, and any one who proposed to reduce it by half would be difficult to answer. The evidence of Verulam shows that Silchester was not peculiar in the smallness of even its maximum population relatively to its size.

But there was no constant ratio of population to area. Caerwent was less than half the size of Silchester, but it seems to have contained quite as many houses, if not more: judging by the way they stand in the excavated *insulae* there may well have been a hundred in the 44 acres enclosed by the walls. In this Caerwent was perhaps exceptional. It seems to have been laid out as a city almost simultaneously with the neighbouring legionary fortress at Caerleon; in its rectangular plan and in its area it owes something to the model of such a fortress; unlike many Romano-British towns, it had defences from the first, owing, no doubt, to the wildness of the hardly conquered frontier district in which it was planted; and the later growth of population had to accommodate itself as best it could to this pre-existing plan. At Silchester, on the contrary, the defences, even in their earlier form as earthworks, seem designed so as to accommodate themselves to a pre-existing town with streets laid down and houses already spreading along them. Caister-next-Norwich in this respect resembles Caerwent; Cirencester and Wroxeter and London are like Verulam or Silchester. It is certain smaller tribal cities that preserve the fortress-like plan which possibly indicates the existence of defences from the first; and it may be conjectured that in these cases there was the same tendency towards unusual density of population relatively to area.

We may therefore assume an average population of one or two thousand in the smaller tribal capitals, rising to two or three times that number in a place like Wroxeter and even more at Cirencester or Verulam. But even Verulam in the Antonine age is likely to have held, perhaps, nearer 5,000 inhabitants than 10,000; London itself possibly not more than 15,000.

The smallness of these town populations makes it easier to conceive their relation to the life of the country as a whole. Economically, the towns were parasitic on the country-side. They had to be fed by it, and the goods they produced, together with the services they rendered as markets and trading-centres, were no adequate return for the food they consumed and the expenditure which they demanded for the upkeep of their public services. They had their industries; but these consisted only to a small extent in the production of goods needed in the country; most of them were luxury-trades whose produce was mostly used in the towns themselves. They did a large business in retail trade, selling pottery made in Gaul and other imports, but, here again, the total quantity of these goods which found its way into the country districts was the barest fraction of what the towns consumed. From the strictly economic point of view the towns were a luxury. Their function was cultural and political. They stood for the decencies and elegances of civilized life, and they provided a link between the Roman government and the mass of the people, to whom those decencies and elegances were things out of reach. Their populations, rich and poor alike, thus formed a privileged section of the people, privileged to enjoy the blessings of romanization at the expense of the country-folk.

Place-Names

The study of place-names, which has been carried forward systematically and with great learning in England, can reveal many facets of history. It provides, among other things, one approach to the question of continuity between Roman and Anglo-Saxon towns. In France many ancient cities today bear names directly derived from those they bore during the late Roman Empire, which are in turn often derived from the names of the Celtic tribes settled there at the time of the Roman occupation. Paris, for instance, was the capital of the Parisii and Soissons the capital of the Suessiones. Such continuity is usually lacking in England, where fewer places have names reminiscent of those they had before the Germanic conquest. Contrary to the belief of many, a name ending in *-chester* does not necessarily mean that a place was called a *castrum* by the Romans themselves. *Chester* is the modern form of the Old English *ceaster* or *caester*, an early loan word from Latin which meant "a city or walled town, originally one that had been a Roman station." The early English applied it to many Roman settlements, and also to some prehistoric forts that had never been Roman camps.

CHESTER. Known by the geographer Ptolemy as *Dēoua* c. 150 A.D. and as *Deva* in the 4th-century *Itinerarium Antonini*. Bede, c. 730, calls it *civitas Legionum, Legacaestir*, and in British, *Carlegion*. The Anglo-Saxon Chronicle calls it *Legaceaster* in 894 and *Ceaster* in 1094. The name in Domesday Book in 1086 is *Cestre*. *Dēva*, the earliest name, is identical with the river-name Dee, on which Chester lies. The Latin name of Chester must have been *Castra legionum*, which is the source of the Old English *Legacaestir*. Later *Chester* supplanted the longer name *Legacaestir*.

CANTERBURY. The Old British name of Canterbury appears as *Darovernon* in Ptolemy and *Durovernon* in the *Itinerarium Antonini*. Bede records it as *Doruvernis*. In 754 the Anglo-Saxon Chronicle uses the name *Cantwaraburg*, meaning "the burg of the people of Kent." The form *Canterburie* is recorded in 1086.

LINCOLN. The early name of *Lindon* is recorded by Ptolemy, and since the place was a Roman colony, it was called *Lindum colonia* in the seventh century. Bede wrote *Lindocolina* and *Lincolia* appears in Domesday Book.

LONDON. Called *Londinium* by Tacitus in 115–117 A.D., and *Londinion* by Ptolemy. Bede calls it *Lundonia* and the form *Lundenceaster* is used in the Old

Based upon Eilert Ekwall, *The Concise Oxford Dictionary of English Place-Names* (4th edition; Oxford, 1960).

English translation of Bede around 890. The Anglo-Saxon Chronicle usually calls it *Lundene.*

PETERBOROUGH. Originally called *Medeshamstede* ("Mede's homestead") by Bede. In 963 the abbot built a wall around the monastery and therefore called it *Burh,* that is, a borough in the original sense of a fortified place. Since the abbey was dedicated to St. Peter it was later called Peterborough.

SILCHESTER. The British name of this Roman station was *Kalēoua* in Ptolemy and *Calleva* in the *Itinerarium Antonini.* It was called *Silcestre* in Domesday Book.

YORK. The early name *Ebórakon* in Ptolemy, *Eboracum* in Bede was probably derived either from the Celtic personal name *Eburos* or the word for a yew tree, *eburos.* By popular etymology this name changed into *Eoforwīc,* which contains the word for boar, *eofor.* The Old English name was pronounced *Iorvík* by the Scandinavians, and this became *Iork* in Old Norse. From this form the word was re-adopted by the English.

Poetry — "The Ruin"

Poetry and imaginative literature in general provide historians with invaluable evidence about attitudes and interests, but it is evidence which must be interpreted with great care. It is often difficult to determine the date and place of composition, and the conventions and formulas of traditional oral poetry may be misinterpreted as expressions of personal emotion or precise description. Both the difficulties and advantages of poetry as historical evidence are illustrated by the Old English elegy which modern editors have named "The Ruin." Anglo-Saxon poets rarely mention towns or cities, and then usually only to illustrate the mutability of human affairs. "The Ruin" is the only piece of Old English poetry which describes a town in detail, and as luck would have it, a long diagonal burn has destroyed part of the leaf which contains the poem, mutilating the text in the middle and at the end. The manuscript, a collection of poetry, was presented to Exeter Cathedral by Bishop Leofric, who died in 1072, and is known as The Exeter Book. The dialect in which the manuscript is written is late West Saxon; the dialect in which the poem was originally composed seems to be Anglian, possibly West Mercian. Many scholars place the composition in the eighth century, but it is really very difficult to be certain of the date of a poem of this sort, and it may have been composed as late as the tenth century.

Scholars have also disagreed about the subject of "The Ruin." While most think that the poet is writing about the former Roman station at Bath, others have suggested that he had in mind Roman cities in general, or even Hadrian's Wall across the north of England. The number of words and phrases which are otherwise not a part of Old English poetry suggests that the poet was making an effort to describe something he had seen and for which he could find no conventional formulas. The references to tiles and metal-bound walls suggest Roman construction, and the combination of Roman baths and thermal springs is peculiar to the town of Bath. Elaborate arguments should not be based on words which are so rare that their meaning is uncertain, or which are even conjectural readings; the reader is alerted to a number of these uncertainties by question marks in the text. Whatever the specific subject of the poem, it reveals what an Anglo-Saxon thought when he looked upon a Roman ruin and tried to imagine the life of long ago.

This literal translation of "The Ruin," for which I am indebted to Edward B. Irving of the University of Pennsylvania, is based largely on the text and many of the suggested interpretations of R. F. Leslie, *Three Old English Elegies* (Manchester, The University Press, 1961).

Marvellous is this wall-stone; the passing of time has broken it down;
The fortified places (*burgstede*) have fallen asunder; the works of giants crumble.
Roofs have fallen, towers have tumbled;
The barred gate [?] is plundered; frost is on the mortar;
5 Gaping shelters-against-storms are split open and fallen,
Eaten through by age. The grip of earth will hold
The master-builders [?], [who are] perished, totally lost,
The hard grip of earth, until a hundred generations
Of men will have gone by.[1] Often this wall endured,
10 Lichen-grey [?] and red-stained, [still] powerful after the others [fell],
Remained standing under storms. [Then] high and curved it fell.
The . . . still totters . . . . cut
Penetrated . . . .
Fiercely sharpened . . . .
15 . . . . shone . . . .
. . . . clever work decreed long ago . . .
. . . . . . sagged in mud-crusts [?].
The mind suggested [?], set in motion a swift intention;
An intelligent brave man bound into rings
20 The wall-edges [?] marvellously with wires.
The buildings were bright, the halls[2] many,
Lofty gabled monuments, great uproar of soldiery,
Many a mead-hall full of human joys,
Until strong Fate changed all that.
25 Great numbers fell dead, the plague-days came;
Death took away all the brave men.
Their fortress turned into deserted foundations.
The fortified place (*burgsteall*) crumbled. Those soldiers who would have mended it
Had fallen dead to earth. Therefore those buildings decayed,
30 And the red curved inner vault [??] of the roof [?]
Parts with its tiles.[3] Ruin has fallen to earth,
Crumbled into mounds, where once long ago many a warrior,
Glad-hearted and gold-bright, splendidly dressed,
Swashbuckling and drunk with wine, shone in his armor.
35 He looked at treasure and silver, at finely worked jewels,
At wealth and property, at a precious stone,
In this bright fortified place (*burg*) of the broad kingdom.
The stone-buildings stood; the stream threw out widely
A hot wave; the wall included it all
40 In its bright embrace; there the baths were,
Hot in the interior; that was convenient.
They let flow then . . . .
Over the grey stone hot streams
. . . .
45 Up to the ring-pool.[4] Hot . . . .

[1] Presumably until Doomsday.
[2] Possibly bath-halls.
[3] This sentence contains unusual vocabulary. In contrast, the next two sentences are quite conventional.
[4] This compound is unique in Old English. At Roman Bath there was a large circular bath next to the rectangular Great Bath.

. . . . where the baths were.
Then is . . . .
. . . . that is a noble thing,
How the . . . . fortified place (*burg*) . . . .

The Burghal Hidage

Early in the tenth century, probably in the reign of Edward the Elder between 911 and 919, a clerk with an unusual sense of detail compiled a list of the *burhs* of the defensive system of the kingdom of Wessex. For each *burh* he indicated the number of hides, or single family farms, which owed service for the defense of the wall, showing that the defenders ordinarily lived in the surrounding countryside. The text as we have it is corrupt and possibly misleading; the first place mentioned has not been identified, and others are not certain, but archaeological evidence has confirmed the general precision of the record. While some of the *burhs* were newly constructed in the ninth century, archaeological investigations have also shown that others made use of surviving Roman walls, and still others — like Halwell, Pilton and Chisbury (if the identification is correct) — were originally Iron Age hill forts.

To *Eorpeburnan* BELONG 324 hides, to Hastings belong 500 hides, and to Lewes belong 1200 hides, and to Burpham belong 720 hides, to Chichester belong 1500 hides. Then to Portchester belong 650 hides,[1] and to Southampton and to Winchester belong 2400 hides,[2] and to Wilton belong 1400 hides, and to Chisbury (?) belong 500 hides, and to Shaftesbury belong 700 hides, and to Twynham belong 500 hides less 30 hides, and to Wareham belong 1600 hides,[3] and to Bredy (?) belong 800 hides less 40 hides, and to Exeter belong 734 hides, and to Halwell belong 300 hides, and to Lydford belong 150 hides less 10 hides, and to Pilton belong 400 hides less 40 hides, and to Watchet belong 513 hides, and to Axbridge belong 400 hides, and to Lyng belong 100 hides, and to Langport belong 600 hides, and to Bath belong 1000 hides,[4] and 1200 hides belong to Malmesbury, and to Cricklade belong 1400 hides, and 1500 hides to Oxford, and to Wallingford belong 2400 hides,[5] and 1600 hides belong to Buckingham, and to Sashes (?) belong 1000 hides, and 600 hides belong to Eashing, and to Southwark belong 1800 hides.

For the maintenance (?) and defense of an acre's breadth of wall 16 hides are re-

[1] The calculations at the end of the document show that 650 hides would provide for the defense of about 894 yards of wall. The wall of the Roman fort at Portchester measured about 800 yards.

[2] The same formula indicates that 2400 hides would provide for the defense of 3300 yards of wall. The medieval wall of Winchester was about 3240 yards long, containing about 138 acres.

[3] Or 2200 yards, very close to the 2180 yards of medieval wall at Wareham, enclosing between 80 and 90 acres.

[4] Or 1375 yards; the medieval wall at Bath, which probably corresponded closely to the Roman one, was about 1250 yards long.

[5] Like Winchester, about 3300 yards. The fortifications along three sides of Wallingford are about 2115 yards long; the river on the fourth side is about 915 yards.

Based upon A. J. Robertson, *Anglo-Saxon Charters* (2nd ed.; Cambridge, England, 1956), pp. 247–249. Reprinted by permission of Cambridge University Press. For changes see Nicholas Brooks, "The Unidentified Forts of the Burghal Hidage," *Medieval Archaeology*, vol. VII (1964), pp. 74–90.

TENTH-CENTURY BOROUGHS
named in the Burghal Hidage and the Anglo-Saxon Chronicle

quired. If every hide is represented by 1 man, then every pole [i.e. 16½ feet] of wall can be manned by 4 men. Then for the maintenance of 20 poles of wall 80 hides are required, and for a furlong 160 hides are required by the same reckoning as I have stated above. For 2 furlongs 320 hides are required; for 3 furlongs 480 hides. Then for 4 furlongs 640 hides are required. For the maintenance of a circuit of 5 furlongs of wall 800 hides are required. . . . If the circuit is greater, the additional amount can easily be deduced from this account, for 160 men are always required for 1 furlong, then every pole of wall is manned by 4 men.

The Anglo-Saxon Chronicle

Striking events in Anglo-Saxon England were recorded year by year in a number of vernacular annalistic accounts which are known collectively as the *Anglo-Saxon Chronicle.* All seven surviving manuscripts begin with a history of Britain from the invasion by Julius Caesar, and down to the year 891 are based on one account written during the reign of King Alfred. After this point differing annals were written in different places, so that, for instance, some manuscripts contain a detailed account of the activities of Æthelflæd of Mercia ("The Mercian Register"), while others are localized in the south. The chronology of the Chronicle is often discordant or misleading; where possible the dates given here have been corrected. The *Chronicle* is our best source of knowledge about the places occupied by the English and their adversaries the Danes and about when these places were fortified. The strictly military sense of the word "borough" here contrasts with the less precise usage of Domesday Book.

885

IN THIS YEAR the aforesaid army divided into two, one part going east, the other part to Rochester, where they besieged the city [*ceastre*] and made other fortifications round themselves. And nevertheless the English defended the city until King Alfred came up with his army. Then the enemy went to their ships and abandoned their fortification, and they were deprived of their horses there, and immediately that same summer they went back across the sea. . . .

886 That same year King Alfred occupied London; and all the English people that were not under subjection to the Danes submitted to him. And he then entrusted the borough [*burh*] to the control of Ealdorman Ethelred [lord of the Mercians, who married Alfred's daughter Æthelflæd]. . . .

893 The king had divided his army into two, so that always half its men were at home, half on service, apart from the men who guarded the boroughs. . . . Then the English forces besieged them [the Danes] there for as long as their provisions lasted; but they had completed their term of service and used up their provisions, and the king was then on the way there with the division which was serving with him. When he was on his way there and the other English army was on its way home, and the Danes were remaining behind there because their king had been wounded in the battle, so that they could not move him, those Danes who lived in Northumbria and East Anglia collected some hundred ships, and went south round the coast. And

some 40 ships went north around the coast and besieged a fortress on the north coast of Devon, and those who had gone south besieged Exeter. When the king heard that, he turned west towards Exeter with the whole army, except for a very inconsiderable portion of the people [who continued] eastwards. They went on until they came to London, and then with the citizens [*burhware*] and with the reinforcements which came to them from the west, they went east to Benfleet. . . . Haesten had previously built that fortress at Benfleet; and he was then out on a raid, and the large army was at home. Then the English went there and put the enemy to flight, and stormed the fortress and captured all that was within, both goods, and women and also children, and brought all to London; and they either broke up or burnt all the ships, or brought them to London or to Rochester. . . .

894 And when the Danish army which had besieged Exeter turned homewards, they ravaged up in Sussez near Chichester, and the citizens [*burhware*] put them to flight and killed many hundreds of them, and captured some of their ships. . . .

911 In this year Ethelred, ealdorman of the Mercians, died, and King Edward succeeded to London and Oxford and to all the lands which belonged to them.

912 In this year about Martinmas [Nov. 11], King Edward ordered the northern borough at Hertford to be built, between the Maran, the Beane, and the Lea, and then after that in the summer, between Rogation days and midsummer [i.e., between May 18 and June 24], King Edward went with some of his forces into Essex to Maldon, and camped there while the borough was being made and constructed at Witham,[1] and a good number of the people who had been under the rule of the Danish men submitted to him. And meanwhile some of his forces made the borough at Hertford on the south side of the Lea.

[1] The borough at Witham had an inner enclosure containing 9½ acres and an outer enclosure, perhaps for cattle, of over 26 acres.

913 In this year the [Danish] army from Northampton and Leicester rode out after Easter and broke the peace, and killed many men at Hook Norton and round about there. . . .

Then the men from Hereford and Gloucester and from the nearest boroughs met them [the Danish army] and fought against them and put them to flight and killed the earl Hroald and the brother of Ohter, the other earl, and a great part of the army. . . .

And then after that in the same year, before Martinmas, King Edward went to Buckingham with his army, and stayed there four weeks, and made both the boroughs, on each side of the river, before he went away. And Earl Thurcetel came and accepted him as his lord, and so did all the earls and the principal men who belonged to Bedford, and also many of those who belonged to Northampton.

915 In this year King Edward went with his army to Bedford, before Martinmas, and obtained the borough; and almost all the citizens, who dwelt there before, submitted to him. And he stayed there four weeks, and before he went away ordered the borough on the south side of the river to be built.

916 In this year, before midsummer, King Edward went to Maldon and built and established the borough before he went away.[2] And that same year Earl Thurcetel went across the sea to France, along with the men who were willing to serve him, with King Edward's peace and support.

917 In this year before Easter King Edward ordered the borough at Towcester to be occupied and built;[3] and then after that in the same year at the Rogation days he ordered the borough at *Wigingamere* to be built. That same summer, between Lammas and midsummer [June 24–Aug. 1], the army from Northampton and Leicester and north of these places broke the peace, and went to Towcester, and fought all day against the borough. . . .

[2] Maldon is reported to have contained about 22 acres.

[3] Towcester was about 35 acres large.

Then after that during the same summer a great host assembled in King Edward's dominions from the nearest boroughs which could manage it and went to Tempsford and besieged the borough and attacked it until they took it by storm; and they killed the king and Earl Toglos and his son Earl Manna, and his brother and all those who were inside and chose to defend themselves; and they captured the others and everything that was inside.

And afterwards, very soon after that, a great [English] host assembled in autumn, both from Kent, from Surrey, from Essex and from the nearest boroughs on all sides; and they went to Colchester and besieged the borough and attacked it until they took it and killed all the people and seized everything that was inside — except the men who fled there over the wall. . . .

Then very soon afterwards in the same autumn King Edward went with the army of the West Saxons to Passenham, and stayed there while the borough of Towcester was provided with a stone wall. And Earl Thurferth and the *holds*[4] submitted to him, and so did all the army which belonged to Northampton, as far north as the Welland, and sought to have him as their lord and protector. . . .

Moreover, after that during the same year, before Martinmas, King Edward went with the army of the West Saxons to Colchester, and repaired and restored the borough where it had been broken. And many people who had been under the rule of the Danes both in East Anglia and in Essex submitted to him; and all the army in East Anglia swore agreement with him, that they would [agree to] all that he would, and would keep peace with all with whom the king wished to keep peace, both at sea and on land. And the army which belonged to Cambridge[5] chose him especially as its lord and protector, and established it with oaths just as he decreed it.

918 In this year, between Rogation days and midsummer, King Edward went with the army to Stamford, and ordered the borough on the south side of the river to be built; and all the people who belonged to the more northern borough submitted to him and sought to have him as their lord. Then during the stay he made there, his sister Æthelflæd died at Tamworth twelve days before midsummer. And then he occupied the borough of Tamworth, and all the nation in the land of the Mercians which had been subject to Æthelflæd submitted to him; and the kings in Wales, Hywel, Clydog, and Idwal, and all the race of the Welsh, sought to have him as lord.

Then he went from there to Nottingham, and captured the borough and ordered it to be repaired and manned both with Englishmen and Danes.[6] And all the people who had settled in Mercia, both Danish and English, submitted to him.

919 In this year after autumn King Edward went with the army to Thelwall and ordered the borough to be built, occupied and manned; and while he stayed there he ordered another army, also from the people of Mercia, to occupy Manchester in Northumbria, and repair and man it.

920 In this year, before midsummer, King Edward went with the army to Nottingham, and ordered to be built the borough on the south side of the river, opposite the other, and the bridge over the Trent between the two boroughs.

Then he went from there into the Peak district to Bakewell, and ordered a borough to be built in the neighbourhood and manned. . . .

1002 In this year the king and his councillors determined that tribute should be paid to the [Danish] fleet and peace made with them on condition that they should cease their evil-doing. Then the king sent Ealdorman Leofsige to the fleet, and he then, by the command of the king and his councillors, arranged a truce with them and that they should receive provisions

[4] A Scandinavian term for a noble with a wergeld double that of a thegn.

[5] The borough at Cambridge, originally Danish, contained about 30 acres.

[6] This originally Danish borough contained about 39 acres.

and tribute. And they then accepted that, and 24,000 pounds were paid them. . . .

1007 In this year the tribute was paid to the army, namely 36,000 pounds. . . .

The Mercian Register

912 In this year Æthelflæd, lady of the Mercians, came on the holy eve of the Invention of the Cross [May 2] to Scergeat, and built the borough there, and in the same year that at Bridgnorth.

913 In this year, by the grace of God, Æthelflæd, lady of the Mercians, went with all the Mercians to Tamworth, and built the borough there in the early summer, and afterwards, before Lammas [Aug. 1], that at Stafford.

914 Then afterwards in the next year, that at Eddisbury[7] in the early summer, and later in the same year, in the early autumn, that at Warwick.

915 Then afterwards in the next year after Christmas, that at Chirbury and that at *Weardbyrig;* and in the same year before Christmas, that at Runcorn. . . .

917 In this year, Æthelflæd, lady of the Mercians, with the help of God, before Lammas obtained the borough which is called Derby, with all that belongs to it; and there also four of her thegns, who were dear to her, were killed within the gates.

918 In this year, with God's help, she peacefully obtained control of the borough of Leicester, in the early part of the year; and the greater part of the army which belonged to it was subjected. And also the people of York had promised her — and some had given pledges, some had confirmed it with oaths — that they would be under her direction. But very soon after they had agreed to this, she died twelve days before midsummer in Tamworth, in the eighth year in which with lawful authority she was holding dominion over the Mercians. And her body is buried in Gloucester in the east chapel of St. Peter's church.

[7] Eddisbury contained about 10 acres.

Laws

The laws or dooms, as they are sometimes called, of the kings who reigned in England are a source of knowledge which has great value, but which must be carefully evaluated. Most law in the early middle ages was customary law; that is, ancient, established practice had the force of law, and the legislative work of a ruler and his court consisted of making public what well-informed men knew to be the law. Such customary law is evidence of the stated practices of the people concerned. Some Germanic monarchs, however, issued laws similar to those of the Roman emperors or a modern legislature. These laws are direct evidence only of how the ruler wished things to be, and may be indirect evidence that matters were actually quite different. For instance, the provisions in the laws of King Athelstan that all major business transactions and minting of coins must take place in a town show us the king's will to control such affairs in his boroughs, but the laws themselves show us nothing of his powers of enforcement.

The following extracts are the most important provisions relating to towns and commerce in the early laws. To read them in extracted form may have the misleading effect of suggesting that they are typical of the laws as a whole.

The complete codes, which are usually quite short and make fascinating reading, reveal a society far more concerned with agriculture, cattle-raising, fighting, and religion, rather than commerce or town-life.

From the Laws of Hlothere and Eadric, Kings of Kent (673–685?)

If a man of Kent buys property (*feoh*)[1] in London, he shall have two or three trustworthy men, or the king's town-reeve (*wicgerefan*), as witness.

16.1. If afterwards it is claimed from the man in Kent, he shall summon as witness, to the king's residence in London, the man who sold it him, if he knows him and can produce him as warrant for the transaction.

16.2. If he cannot do so, he shall declare on the altar, with one of his witnesses or with the king's town-reeve, that he bought the property openly in London, and with goods known to be his, and the value [of the property] shall be returned to him.

Extract from King Athelstan's Laws Issued at Grately[2]

12. And we have declared that no one shall buy goods worth more than 20 pence [the value of a cow] outside a town (*port*), but he shall buy within the town, in the presence of the town-reeve (*portgerefan*) or some other trustworthy man, or again, in the presence of the reeves at a public meeting.

13. And we declare that every borough shall be repaired by a fortnight after Rogation days [in the fifth week after Easter].

13.1. Secondly, that all trading shall be carried on in a town.

14. Thirdly, that there shall be one coinage throughout the king's realm, and no man shall mint money except in a town.

14.1. And if a moneyer is found guilty [of issuing base or light coins], the hand shall be cut off with which he committed the crime, and fastened up on the mint. But if he is accused and wishes to clear himself, then he shall go to the [ordeal of] hot iron and redeem the hand with which he is accused of having committed the crime. And if he is proved guilty the same punishment shall be inflicted as we have already declared.

14.2. In Canterbury there shall be seven moneyers: four for the king, two for the archbishop, one for the abbot [of St. Augustine's]; in Rochester two for the king and one for the bishop; in London eight; in Winchester six; in Lewes two; in Hastings one; another in Chichester; two in Southampton; two in Wareham; one in Dorchester; two in Exeter; two at Shaftesbury; and one in [each of] the other boroughs. . . .[3]

20. And if anyone fails to attend an assembly three times, he shall pay the fine due to the king for insubordination. And the meeting of the assembly shall be announced seven days before it is held.

20.1. If, however, he will not comply with the law, and pay the fine for insubordination, then all the chief men who belong to the borough shall ride [to his house] and take all that he owns, and place him under surety.

Extract from King Edgar's Laws Issued at Andover (?)[4]

5. And the hundred court shall be attended as has been previously ordained.

5.1. And the borough court shall be held three times in the year and the shire court twice.

5.2. And the bishop of the diocese and the ealdorman shall be present, and shall direct the observance of both ecclesiastical and secular law.

[1] *Feoh* may mean either "cattle" or "property."
[2] II Athelstan, 924–939.
[3] See map on p. 58. [Editor's note.]
[4] III Edgar, 959–963.

Extract from King Edgar's Laws Issued at "Wihtbordesstan" [5]

2.2. The following measure shall apply generally to the whole nation — to the English, Danes and Britons in every part of my dominion — to the end that rich and poor may possess what they have lawfully acquired; and that thieves, even if they steal anything, may not know where to deposit their stolen goods; and that, little as they may like it, such precautions be taken against them that very few of them may escape.

3. My will is, further, that every man be under surety, whether he live within a borough or in the country.

3.1. And a body of standing witnesses shall be appointed for every borough and for every hundred.

4. 36 persons shall be chosen as witnesses for every borough;

5. 12 for small boroughs and for every hundred, unless you desire more.

6. And every man shall buy and sell in the presence of these witnesses all the goods which he buys or sells either in a borough or in a *wapentake* [the equivalent of a hundred in the north of England].

6.1. And each of them, when he is first chosen as a witness, shall swear an oath that he will never, for money or favor or fear, deny any of the things of which he has been witness, or declare in his testimony anything except only what he has seen or heard.

6.2. And two or three men who have taken the oath in this manner shall be present as witnesses at every transaction.

7. And he who rides out to make any purchase shall inform his neighbors of the object of his journey; and when he comes home, he shall also declare who was present as witness when he bought the goods.

8. If, however, he makes a purchase unexpectedly, when he is away on some journey or other, and he had not given notice of it when he set out, he shall do so when he comes home; and, if it is livestock, he shall bring it to the common pasture with the cognisance of the village to which he belongs.

Customary Practice Concerning Status [6]

1. Once it used to be that people and rights went by dignities, and councillors of the people were then entitled to honor, each according to his rank, whether noble or *ceorl,* retainer or lord.

2. And if a *ceorl* prospered, that he possessed fully five hides of land of his own, a bell and a castle-gate (*burhgeat*), a seat and special office in the king's hall, then was he henceforth entitled to the rights of a thegn.

3. And the thegn who prospered, that he served the king and rode in his household band on his missions, if he himself had a thegn who served him, possessing five hides on which he discharged the king's dues, and who attended his lord in the king's hall, and had thrice gone on his errand to the king — then he was afterwards allowed to represent his lord with his preliminary oath, and legally obtain his [right to pursue a] charge, wherever he needed.

4. And he who had no such distinguished representative, swore in person to obtain his rights, or lost his case.

5. And if a thegn prospered, that he became an earl, then was he afterwards entitled to an earl's rights.

6. And if a trader prospered, that he crossed thrice the open sea at his own expense, he was then afterwards entitled to the rights of a thegn.

7. And if there were a scholar who prospered with his learning so that he took orders and served Christ, he should afterwards be entitled to so much more honor and protection as belonged by rights to that order, if he kept himself [chaste] as he should.

8. And if anyone, anywhere, injured an ecclesiastic or a stranger by word or deed, then it was the concern of the bishop and the king, that they should atone for it as quickly as they could.

[5] IV Edgar, 962–963.

[6] Probably a private compilation made early in the eleventh century.

Numismatics

A. Edward the Elder (899–924). From an unidentified northwestern mint. Obverse: EADWEARD REX. Reverse: Moneyer's name ATHULF irregularly written. The right hand of God appears on many coins, and brings to mind the punishment for fraudulent coinage (II Athelstan 14.1, p. 54).

B. Aethelred II (978–1016). Obv.: + AEÐELRED REX ANGLO[RUM]. Rev.: AELFNOÐ MO[NETARIUS] EAXE[CEASTER], Aelfnoth the moneyer at Exeter.

C. Ceolnoth, Archbp. of Canterbury (833–870). Obv.: CEOLNOÐ ARCHIEP. (note tonsure on figure). Rev.: BIARNRED MONETA[RIUS]. Biarnred the moneyer.

The careful study of thousands of surviving Anglo-Saxon coins has permitted specialists (known as numismatists) to establish much precise information. The silver pennies (*denarii*) commonly used during the late Anglo-Saxon period can be dated by the name of the king which appears on them, since only a few other magnates, such as the Archbishop of Canterbury, ever acquired the authority to issue money in England. Since the coiner who actually minted the money was responsible for its quality, his name usually appeared on the coins too. During the tenth century it became increasingly common for the coins also to bear the name of the place at which they were minted. Identifications of mints are sometimes very difficult, but a reasonably accurate list showing where coins were issued during different reigns can be established; further research and discoveries may of course add to this list. Marking on the map the early mints, say those coining before 978, helps to answer the question of why further mints were added; by 1066 there was a mint within half a day's walk of practically every farm in England. To rate the comparative importance of mints other than by the number of moneyers (see II Athelstan 14.2, p. 54) is more difficult. One problem, for instance, is that many coins were shipped from England to Scandinavia as tribute, and the most important mints of the two regions, London and Lund, used the same mint signature. A very rough ranking is that something under one fourth of all late Saxon pence were struck at London, about a tenth at York, slightly less at Lincoln, and perhaps one in 15 at Winchester. Canterbury, Exeter, Norwich, Stamford,

Based upon J. J. North, *English Hammered Coinage,* vol. I (London, 1963), pp. 172–185. Reprinted by permission of Spink & Sons, Ltd., and of the author.

Thetford, Chester and Leicester come next, among them striking about as many coins as London, and all the other mints combined produced a final quarter of the coinage. The counties are listed here in the order followed by Domesday Book (see pp. 67ff.).

Mints and Their Issues

Kings of Wessex

Al Alfred (871–899)
EdE Edward the Elder (899–924)
Athn Athelstan (924–939)
Edm Edmund (939–946)
Edr Edred (946–955)

Kings of England

Edw Edwig (955–959)
Edg Edgar (959–975)
EdM Edward the Martyr (975–978)
Ethd II Ethelred II (978–1016)
Cn Cnut (1016–1035)
Hd I Harold I (joint king 1035–37, sole king 1037–40)
Hcn Harthacnut (joint king 1035–37, sole king 1040–42)
EdC Edward the Confessor (1042–1066)
Hd II Harold II (Jan.–Oct. 1066)

Kent

1. Canterbury: Al, Athn, Edg to Hd II.
2. Dover: Athn, Ethd II to Hd II.
3. Hythe: EdC.
4. Lympne: Edg, EdM, Ethd II, Cn.
5. Rochester: Athn, Edg to Hd II.
6. Romney: Ethd II to Hd II.
7. Sandwich: EdC.

Sussex

8. Chichester: Athn, Edg, Ethd II to Hd II.
9. Cissbury: Ethd II, Cn.
10. Hastings: Ethd II to Hd II.
11. Lewes: Athn, Edg to Hd II.
12. Steyning: Cn to Hd II.

Surrey

13. Guildford: EdM, Ethd II to Hd II.
14. Southwark: Ethd II, Cn, Hd I, EdC, Hd II.

Hampshire

15. Southampton: Athn, Edw, Edg?, EdM?, Ethd II, Cn, Hd I.
16. Winchester: Al, Athn, Edw to Hd II.

Berkshire

17. Reading: EdC.
18. Wallingford: Athn, Edg, Ethd II to Hd II.

Wiltshire

19. Bedwyn: EdC.
20. Cricklade: Ethd II to Hd II.
21. Malmesbury: Edg, Ethd II to Hd II.
22. Salisbury: Ethd II to EdC.
23. Warminster: Ethd II, Cn, Hd I, EdC.
24. Wilton: Edg to Hd II.

Dorsetshire

25. Bridport: Ethd II, Cn, Hcn, EdC.
26. Dorchester: Ethd II to EdC.
27. Shaftesbury: Athn, Edg, Ethd II to Hd II.

Somersetshire

28. Axbridge: Ethd II, Cn, Hcn.
29. Bath: EdE, Athn, Edm, Edw to Hd II.
30. Bruton: Ethd II, Cn.
31. Cadbury: Ethd II, Cn.
32. Crewkerne: Ethd II, Cn, Hd I.
33. Frome?: Cn, Hcn, EdC.
34. Ilchester: Edg to EdC.
35. Langport: Athn, Cn to EdC.
36. Milborne port: Ethd II, Cn.
37. Petherton: EdC.
38. Taunton: Ethd II, Cn, Hcn, EdC, Hd II.
39. Watchet: Ethd II to EdC.

Devonshire

40. Barnstaple: Edw, Ethd II, Cn, Hd I, EdC.

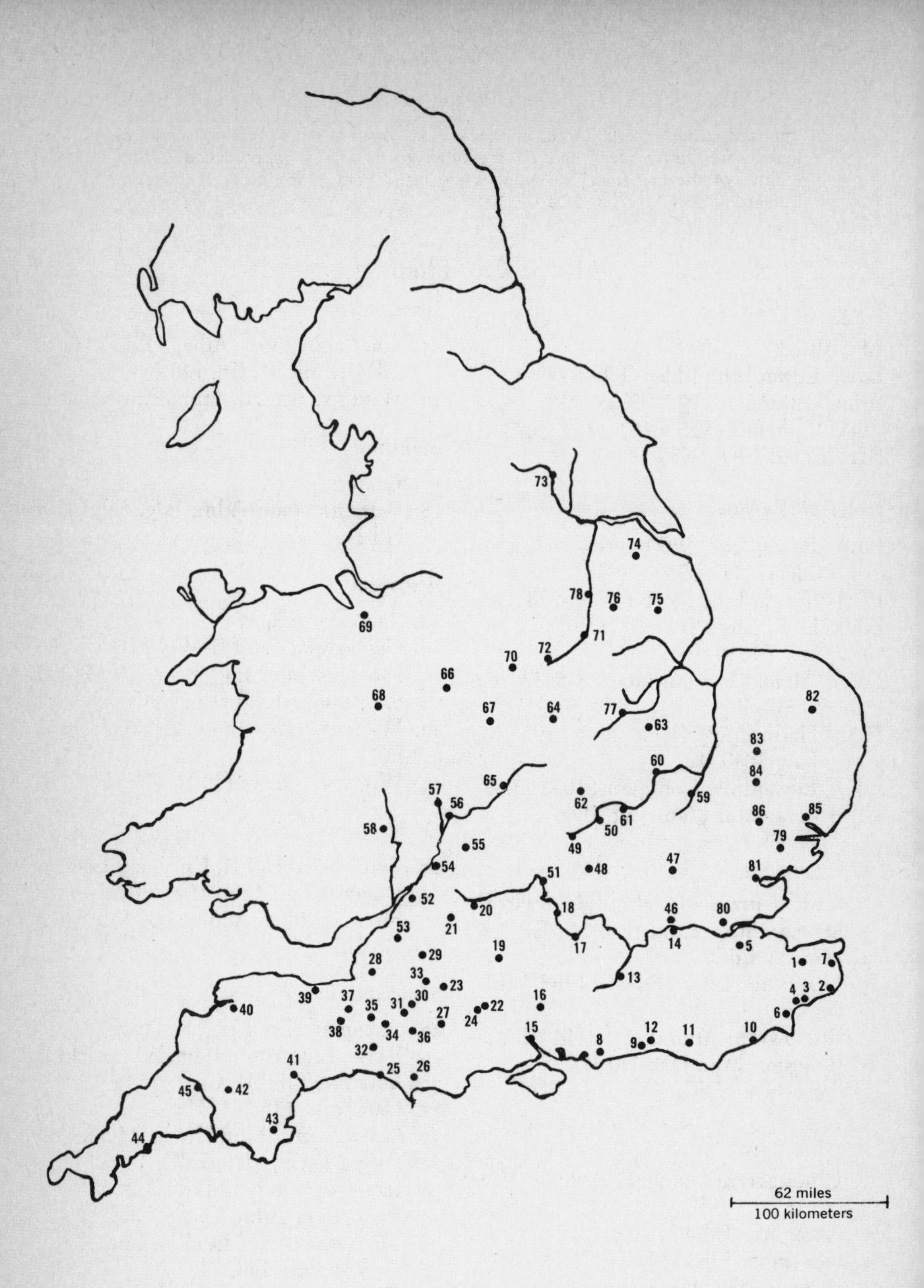

ANGLO-SAXON MINTS

41. Exeter: Al, Athn, Edg to Hd II.
42. Lydford: EdM to Cn, Hd I, EdC.
43. Totnes: Athn?, Edw to Cn.

Cornwall

44. Castle Gotha?: Ethd II to Hcn.
45. Launceston: Ethd II.

Middlesex

46. London: Al, Athn, Edw to Hd II.

Hertfordshire

47. Hertford: Athn, Edw to Hd I, EdC.

Buckinghamshire

48. Aylesbury: Ethd II, Cn, EdC.
49. Buckingham: EdM, Ethd II to EdC.
50. Newport Pagnell: EdM?, EdC.

Oxfordshire

51. Oxford: Athn, Edr, Edg to Hd II.

Gloucestershire

52. Berkeley: EdC.
53. Bristol: Ethd II? to Hd II.
54. Gloucester: Al, Athn, Edg to Hd II.
55. Winchcombe: Edg, Ethd II, Cn, Hcn, EdC, Hd II.

Worcestershire

56. Pershore: EdC.
57. Worcester: Ethd II to Hd I, EdC, Hd II.

Herefordshire

58. Hereford: Athn, Edg, Ethd II to Hd II.

Cambridgeshire

59. Cambridge: Edg to Hd II.

Huntingdonshire

60. Huntingdon: Edw, Edg, Ethd II to Hd II.

Bedfordshire

61. Bedford: Edw to Hd II.

Northamptonshire

62. Northampton: Edw, Edg, EdM?, Ethd II to Hd II.
63. Peterborough: Ethd II, Cn.

Leicestershire

64. Leicester: Athn, Edg, Ethd to Hd II.

Warwickshire

65. Warwick: Athn, Edm to Hd II.

Staffordshire

66. Stafford: Athn, Edg, Ethd II, Hd I, EdC.
67. Tamworth: Athn, Edg to Cn, Hd I, EdC.

Shropshire

68. Shrewsbury: Athn, Edg, Ethd II to Hd II.

Cheshire

69. Chester: Athn, Edm, Edw?, Edg to Hd II.

Derbyshire

70. Derby: Athn, Anlaf II (Viking king of York), Edg to EdC.

Nottinghamshire

71. Newark: Edw?, Ethd II, Cn.
72. Nottingham: Athn, Ethd II to EdC.

Yorkshire

73. York: Athn, Edm?, Viking kings of York, Edg to Hd II.

Lincolnshire

74. Caistor: EdM, Ethd II, Cn?
75. Horncastle: EdM, Ethd II.
76. Lincoln: Edg to Hd II.
77. Stamford: Edg to Hd II.
78. Torksey: EdM, Ethd II, Cn.

Essex

79. Colchester: Ethd II, Cn, Hd I, EdC, Hd II.
80. Horndon: EdC.
81. Maldon: Athn, Edg, Ethd II, Cn, Hd I, EdC, Hd II.

Norfolk

82. Norwich: Athn to Edr, Edg to Hd II.
83. Thetford: Edg to Hd II.

Suffolk

84. BURY ST. EDMUNDS: Athn?, EdC.
85. IPSWICH: Edg to Hd II.
86. SUDBURY: Ethd II, Cn, EdC.

Uncertain town

"DYR," "DERNT" (probably in Suffolk): EdC.

Unknown towns

"NIWAN(PO)": Ethd II } Probably the same mint, which may be BRIDGNORTH, *Shrops.*
"BRYGIN": Ethd II }

"EANBYRI": Cn.
"(D?)ERP": Ethd II.
"ERL": Ethd II.
"WICNEH": Hd II.

Diplomas

Charters, in which a king or other great person recorded grants and obligations in a form more permanent than the memory of mortal witnesses, provide contemporary evidence which is sometimes remarkably precise and detailed. The simpler administrative letters known as writs usually contain less information, but are also a valuable record of the actions and procedures of the king and other lords. Tait's use of the charter of Bishop Eadnoth of Crediton (p. 36) is a good example of the way historical conclusions can be squeezed from such evidence. And the first charter can be applied to the questions arising from Maitland's theory about "appurtenant" burgesses (pp. 23–25). Charters of privileges granted to towns as corporate bodies appear in a later section.

CHARTER OF KING BURGRED OF MERCIA (875)

IN THE NAME of the Lord God Most High, who is the hope of all the ends of the earth and in the sea afar off.

I, indeed, Burgred, by the concession of the most omnipotent God, king of the Mercians, will grant and deliver to Ealhhun my bishop for the relief of my soul with the consent of my counsellors a certain small portion of a liberty, of a profitable little estate in the town of London, *i.e.,* at a place called the haw of Ceolmund, which is situated not far from the west gate; for the bishop to have in his own liberty, or belonging to the city of Worcester, with all the things which rightly belong to it, great and small; *i.e.,* that he is to have therein to use freely the scale and weights and measures as is customary in the port. The liberty of this estate was bought from the king with 60 shillings of silver, and had been purchased before with the same amount of money — one pound — from Ceolmund the "prefect." Peace and security be to all observing this privilege, and may the vengeance of the eternal King fall on those opposing or denying it, if they have not made worthy amends to God and men.

These things were done in the year of our Lord's incarnation 857, and the fifth

The first two selections are from *English Historical Documents,* Vol. I, ed. Dorothy Whitelock (London, 1955), pp. 487–488, 498. Reprinted by permission of Eyre & Spottiswoode Ltd. The third selection is from *Crawford Collection of Early Charters,* ed. A. S. Napier and W. H. Stevenson (Oxford, 1895), pp. 9, 77 (with minor changes). Reprinted by permission of Oxford University Press. The fourth selection is from Florence E. Harmer, *Anglo-Saxon Writs* (Manchester, 1952), p. 234. Reprinted by permission of Manchester University Press. The last two selections are from *English Historical Documents,* Vol. II, ed. David C. Douglas and George W. Greenaway (London, 1953), pp. 968, 970. Reprinted by permission of Eyre & Spottiswoode Ltd.

indiction, in the famous place called Tamworth, on the holy Easter of the Lord. And 12 pence a year is to be paid to the king as rent from that little estate. These were witnesses whose names are here. . . .

Charter of Ethelred and Æthelflæd of Mercia (about 889–899)

To Almighty God, the True Unity and the Holy Trinity in heaven, be praise and honor and thanksgiving for all the benefits which he has granted us. For whose love in the first place, and for that of St. Peter and of the church at Worcester, and also at the request of Bishop Wærferth their friend, Ealdorman Ethelred and Æthelflæd ordered the borough at Worcester to be built for the protection of all the people, and also to exalt the praise of God therein. And they now make known, with the witness of God, in this charter, that they will grant to God and St. Peter and to the lord of that church half of all the rights which belong to their lordship, whether in the market or in the street, both within the fortification and outside; that things may be more honorably maintained in that foundation and also that they may more easily help the community to some extent; and that their memory may be the more firmly observed in that place for ever, as long as obedience to God shall continue in that minster. . . .

And moreover Ethelred and Æthelflæd make known that they will grant this to God and St. Peter with willing heart in the witness of King Alfred and of all the councillors who are in the land of the Mercians; except that the wagon-shilling and the load-penny[1] at Droitwich go to the king as they have always done. But otherwise, land-rent, the fine for fighting, or theft, or dishonest trading, and contribution to the borough-wall, and all the [fines for] offences which admit of compensation, are to belong half to the lord of the church, for the sake of God and St. Peter, exactly as it has been laid down as regards the market-place and the streets. And outside the market-place, the bishop is to be entitled to his land and all his rights, just as our predecessors established and privileged it.

And Ethelred and Æthelflæd did this in the witness of King Alfred and of all the councillors of the Mercians whose names are written hereafter. And they implore all their successors in the name of Almighty God that no one may diminish this charitable gift which they have given to that church for the love of God and St. Peter. . . .

Charter of Bishop Eadnoth of Crediton (about 1018)

I, Bishop Eadnoth, make known in these writs that I borrowed thirty mancuses of gold by lead-weight from Beorhnoth for the redemption of my land, and I delivered to him as security a virgate of land by the Creedy on these conditions, that he should have it for his life, and after his life he should bequeath the money that stands on the land [*i.e.*, the thirty mancuses] to whomsoever he pleases . . . And the bishop made this known to the borough councils [*burhwiton*] at Exeter, and at Totnes, and at Lidford, and at Barnstable.

Writ of Edward the Confessor (1042–44)

King Edward sends friendly greetings to Bishop Ælfweard and Wulfgar my port-reeve [*portgerefa*] and all the citizens [*burhware*] in London. And I inform you

[1] The payments on a cart-load or pack-load of salt.

that my will is that my men in the gild of English *cnihtas* shall be entitled to their sac and their soc within borough and without over their lands and over their men. And my will is that they shall enjoy as good laws as they enjoyed in the days of King Edgar and in my father's days and similarly in Cnut's. And I will moreover augment its benefits. And I will not permit anyone to do them any wrong, but [on the contrary] may they all prosper! And God keep you all.

Writ of Robert of Meulan for the Merchants of Leicester (1103–1118)

Robert, count of Meulan, to Ralph the butler, and all his barons, both French and English, of all his lands of England, greeting. Know that I have granted to all my merchants of Leicester their gild-merchant with all the customs by which they held it in the time of King William and King William, his son, and which they now hold in the time of King Henry. Witness: Robert, son of Alcitil.

Writ of Henry II for the Gild-Merchant of Lincoln (1154–1160)

Henry, king of the English, and duke of the Normans and of the men of Aquitaine, count of the Angevins, to the bishop of Lincoln and to the justice and sheriff and the barons of Lincoln and of Lincolnshire, greeting. I order that no merchant who is a stranger and from outside shall be resident in Lincoln for the purpose of dyeing his cloths or of selling by retail, except those who are in the gild, and who contribute to the customs of the town, and who pay my geld with the inhabitants as they were wont to do in the time of King Henry. Witness: Reginald, earl of Cornwall; Henry of Essex, the constable; Richard of Le Hommet.

The Billingsgate Tolls

The tolls to be collected at the Billingsgate quay of the port of London are recorded in a document from the early part of the eleventh century which has the form of a set of royal ordinances, though the name of no king is given. Both the cosmopolitan and the rural character of the London market are readily apparent.

If a small ship came to Billingsgate, 1 half-penny was paid as toll; if a larger ship with sails, 1 penny was paid.

1. If a barque or a merchantman arrives and lies there, 4 pence is paid as toll.
2. From a ship with a cargo of planks, one plank is given as toll.
3. On three days of the week toll for cloth [is paid] — on Sunday and Tuesday and Thursday.
4. A merchant who came to the bridge [*i.e.*, Old London Bridge] with a boat containing fish paid 1 half-penny as toll, and for a larger ship 1 penny.
5. Men of Rouen, who came with wine or blubber fish, paid a duty of 6 shillings for a large ship and 5% of the fish.
6. Men from Flanders and Ponthieu and Normandy and the Isle of France exhibited their goods and paid toll.

From A. J. Robertson, *Laws of the Kings of England* (Cambridge, England, 1925), pp. 71–73. Reprinted by permission of Cambridge University Press.

7. Men from Huy and Liège and Nivelles who were passing through [London] paid a sum for exhibition and toll.

8. And subjects of the Emperor who came in their ships were entitled to the same privileges as ourselves.

9. Besides wool, which had been unloaded, and melted fat, they were also permitted to buy three live pigs for their ships.

10. But they were not allowed any right of pre-emption over the burgesses [*burhmanni*], and [they had] to pay their toll, and at Christmas two lengths of grey cloth and one length of brown and 10 pounds of pepper and five pairs of gloves and two saddle-kegs of vinegar, and the same at Easter.

11. From hampers with hens, one hen [is given] as toll, and from one hamper of eggs, five eggs as toll, if they come to the market.

12. Women who deal in dairy produce [*i.e.*, cheese and butter] pay 1 penny a fortnight before Christmas, and another penny a week before Christmas.

Gild Documents

A medieval gild was an association for mutual assistance, a sort of fraternity. Its members regularly ate and drank together, and in early usage the word "gild" meant ritual conviviality and drink. The modern practice of restricting the word to associations of merchants and artisans is too narrow, for medieval men of all sorts formed gilds as naturally as their descendants establish committees. In a book which overturned the popular theory that town governments had grown from gilds, Charles Gross (1857–1909), then an instructor at Harvard, wrote "In the sources for the history of the Anglo-Saxon period there is no trace of the existence of the Gild Merchant, or of any gilds forming the nucleus of town government, or even participating in the latter." [1] More recently it has been argued that Gross drew his distinctions too sharply, that gilds of which merchants were members existed before the conquest, and that although town governments and gilds were separate entities, the practical effects of overlapping interests and memberships should not be discounted. Besides the documents which follow, three pieces concerning gilds are included in the section on diplomas (pp. 61–62).

Regulations of the Thegns' Gild in Cambridge (11th century)

Here in this writing is the declaration of the enactment which this fellowship has determined in the thegns' gild in Cambridge.

1. Firstly, that each was to give to the other an oath of true loyalty, in regard to religious and secular affairs, on the relics; and all the fellowship was ever to aid him who had most right.

2. If any gild-brother die, all the gildship is to bring him to where he desired, and he who does not come for that purpose is to

[1] *The Gild Merchant* (Oxford, 1890), p. 2.

The first selection is from *English Historical Documents,* vol. I, ed. Dorothy Whitelock (London, 1955), pp. 557–558. The second selection is from *English Historical Documents,* vol. II, ed. David C. Douglas and George W. Greenaway (London, 1953), pp. 950–951. Reprinted by permission of Eyre & Spottiswoode Ltd. The last selection is from Charles Gross, *The Gild Merchant,* vol. II (Oxford, 1890), pp. 116–123. Translated by the editor.

pay a sester of honey;[1] and the gildship is to supply half the provisions for the funeral feast in honor of the deceased; and each is to contribute two pence for the almsgiving, and from it the fitting amount is to be brought to St. Æthelthryth's [at Ely].

3. And if then any gild-brother have any need of his fellows' help and it is made known to the reeve of the nearest gild-brother — unless the gild-brother himself be at hand — and the reeve neglects it, he is to pay one pound.

4. If the lord neglects it, he is to pay one pound, unless he is engaged on the necessary business of his lord, or is on a bed of sickness.

5. And if anyone kill a gild-brother, nothing other than eight pounds is to be accepted as compensation.

6. If the slayer scorn to pay the compensation, all the gildship is to avenge the gild-brother and all bear the feud.

7. If then one avenges him, all are to bear the feud alike.

8. And if any gild-brother slays a man and does it as an avenger by necessity and to remedy the insult to him, and the slain man's wergild is 1,200 [shillings], each gild-brother is to supply half a mark to his aid; if the slain man is a *ceorl,* two ores; if he is servile [or Welsh?], one ore.

9. If, however, the gild-brother kill anyone foolishly and wantonly, he is himself to be responsible for what he has done.

10. And if a gild-brother slay a gild-brother through his own folly, he is himself to be responsible towards the kindred for the offence he has committed, and to buy back his membership of the gild with eight pounds, or he is to forfeit for ever fellowship and friendship.

11. And if a gild-brother eats or drinks with the man who slew his gild-brother — unless it be in the presence of the king, or the bishop of the diocese, or the ealdorman — he is to pay one pound, unless he can deny with two of his bench-fellows that he knew him.

12. If any gild-brother insult another, he is to pay a sester of honey, unless he can clear himself with two of his bench-fellows.

13. If a retainer draws a weapon, the lord is to pay one pound, and the lord is to get from him what he can, and all the gildship is to assist him to recover his money.

14. And if a retainer wound another, the lord is to avenge it, and all the gildship together; that — no matter what advocacy he seek — he shall not keep his life.

15. And if a retainer sits within the dais [?] he is to pay a sester of honey.

16. And if anyone has a *fotsetla* [an attendant at his feet?], he is to do the same.

17. And if any gild-brother dies outside the district, or is taken ill, his gild-brothers are to fetch him and bring him, dead or alive, to where he wishes, on pain of the same fine which has been stated in the event of his dying at home and a gild-brother failing to attend the body.

18. And the gild-brother who does not attend his morning conference is to pay his sester of honey.

Extract from the Narrative of the Benefactions of an Augustinian Priory in London

In the year of the Incarnation of our Lord 1125, certain burgesses of London, from that old descent of noble English knights, coming together in the chapter of Christ Church, which is situate within the walls of the city next to the gate which is called Aldgate, gave to this same church and the canons who there served God all the land and jurisdiction which is in English described as belonging to the English *cnihtengild,*[2] and which stretches from outside the wall of the city by the same gate as far as the river Thames. The names of the burgesses who did this were Ralph, son of Algod; Wulward "le Doverisshe";

[1] Mead is a mixture of fermented honey and water. [Editor's note.]

[2] See glossary. [Editor's note.]

Ordgar "le Prude"; Edward Upcornhill; Blackstan and Ailwin, his cousin; Ailwin and Robert, his brother, the sons of Leofstan; Leofstan the goldsmith and Wyzo, his son; Hugh, son of Wulfgar; Algar Fecusenne; Ordgar, son of Deorman; Osbert Drenchwyn; Adelard Hornewitesune. They made their gift, I say, and became members of the fraternity and sharers in the benefits of that place by the hand of Norman the prior who received them and their predecessors into the society on the text of the Holy Gospel. And that this gift should remain firm and unbroken they offered on the altar the charter of St. Edward which they had,[3] together with their other charters. . . .

Record of an Election at Ipswich (1200)

On Thursday after the feast of the Nativity of St. John the Baptist in the second year of the reign of King John [June 29, 1200] the whole community of the borough of Ipswich gathered in the cemetery of St. Mary at the Tower to choose two bailiffs and four coroners in the same borough, following the procedure of the charter of the aforementioned lord king which the king recently granted to the burgesses of the said borough. At this time the burgesses unanimously and by common assent chose two upright and lawful men of their community, namely John Fitz-Norman and William of Belines, who were sworn to take charge of the reeveship of the borough, and that they will properly and faithfully treat both poor and rich.

Also on the same day they unanimously chose four coroners, namely John Fitz-Norman, William of Belines, Philip of the Gate, and Roger Lew, who were sworn to take charge of the pleas of the crown and to do those other things in the town which pertain to the crown, and see that the aforementioned bailiffs justly and lawfully treat both poor and rich.

Also on the same day it was ordained by the common counsel of the community that in addition twelve capital portmen [*capitales portmenni*] shall be sworn in the borough, as there are in other free boroughs of England, and that they shall have full power [*plena potestas*], for themselves and the whole community, to govern and maintain the borough and all the liberties of the borough, and to render the judgments of the town, and also to take charge of and ordain and do all those things in the borough which ought to be done for the well-being and honor of the town. And on this matter the bailiffs and coroners declared that all the community should come to the cemetery on Sunday after the coming feast of the apostles Peter and Paul to choose the 12 capital portmen following the provisions of the same ordinance.

On Sunday after the feast of the apostles Peter and Paul [July 2], the whole community of Ipswich gathered in the presence of the bailiffs and coroners of the town, as was earlier ordained. And the bailiffs and coroners with the assent of the community chose four upright and lawful men from each parish of the town who were sworn to choose the 12 capital portmen from the better, more discreet, and more powerful men of the town, to ordain for the well-being of the town, as was said before. And the men who were sworn from each parish came and chose, for themselves and the whole community, these following 12 names: John Fitz-Norman, William of Belines, Philip of the Gate, Roger Lew, Peter Everard, William Goscalk, Amisius Bolle, John of St. George, John le Mayster, Sayer, son of Thurstan, Robert Parys, and Andrew Peper. These men swore in the presence of the whole community that they will properly and faithfully maintain and govern the borough of Ipswich, and to maintain to the best of their ability all the liberties which were recently granted to the burgesses of the borough by the charter of the lord king, and also to maintain all the liberties and free customs of the town,

[3] Printed above, pp. 61–62. [Editor's note.]

and to render justly the judgments of the courts of the town without regard to the person of anyone, and moreover to ordain and do all other things which need to be done for the well-being and honor of the town, and to treat both poor and rich justly and lawfully.

On the same day, as soon as the 12 capital portmen had been sworn in the aforesaid fashion, they made all the community stretch their hands toward the book [i.e., the Gospels] and with one voice solemnly swear that from that hour on they will obey, support, counsel and aid their bailiffs and coroners and each and every capital portman with their bodies and goods to preserve and maintain the town of Ipswich and the new charter and the honor and all the liberties and free customs of the town in all places and against anyone, excepting however against the lord king and the royal power, to the best of their ability, as they ought justly and reasonably to do. . . .

On Thursday after the feast of the Translation of St. Thomas the Martyr [July 13], the bailiffs and coroners and other capital portmen gathered to treat and ordain for the well-being of the town of Ipswich.

First they ordain that the bailiffs and four upright and lawful men of the borough shall collect all the customs of the borough, and that they shall pay annually for the community the proper and customary farm to the exchequer of the lord king.[4]

Also they ordain that an upright and lawful and worthy man shall be chosen in the borough by the common counsel of the community to be alderman of the gild-merchant in the same borough. And that four upright and lawful men of the borough shall be associated with him. And that the alderman and these four shall swear that they will properly and faithfully maintain the gild and everything pertaining to the gild. . . .

Also it was ordained that no burgess of the town shall be quit of the customs of the town for his merchandise, that is, if he be a merchant, unless he is in lot and scot [pays a proportionate share of municipal taxes] for the common aid and business of the town. . . .

On Thursday after the feast of St. Foi in the same year [Oct. 12] . . . an alderman, namely William Gosscalk, was chosen by the common counsel of the community. And four men were chosen to be associated with him, namely Peter Everard, John le Mayster, Roger Lew, and John of St. George, who swore along with the alderman that they will properly and faithfully govern the gild merchant in the borough of Ipswich and all the articles pertaining to the gild. And that they will treat all the brothers of the gild properly and lawfully. And later the alderman and his four associates said in the presence of the people of the town that all who are of the liberty of the town shall come before the alderman and his associates on a certain day, when and where to be made known, to place themselves in the gild and to give an entrance-fee to the gild.

[4] See p. 101. [Editor's note.]

Domesday Book

Domesday Book, a survey of the resources of his kingdom, was prepared for William the Conqueror in 1086. Its two volumes, one of 383 folios and a second (less thoroughly condensed) of 450 folios, contain the most systematic, extensive, and highly detailed record prepared in the early middle ages for any prince north of the shores of the Mediterranean. It is the only surviving document which can be used to estimate the total population of England before the poll tax of 1377. But the clerks, who compiled a record so detailed that men in the twelfth century thought their work comparable to the Book of the Last Judgment, did not have the interests of modern census-takers, did not use standardized vocabulary, and, for one reason or another, omitted information we would like to have. Sometimes they recorded a precise count of the population of the countryside or of towns (or at least of adults or heads of families), in other places of financial returns to the king, in others of the obligations of subjects or the property of feudal vassals. But we have only a blank space for the city of London, which probably had a population of between 10,000 and 20,000; Winchester, which probably rivalled York as the largest city of the realm, is also a blank.

Even when we have details they are fragmentary, difficult to interpret, and tantalizing. Historians have estimated that the total population of England in 1086 was something over one million. But no one can claim precision for estimates based on Domesday figures. Those given here for individual towns are based on the assumption that there were probably an average of four or five people in an urban family or occupying an urban property. The margin of error is here obviously large.

The Domesday commissioners collected information about the condition of England in the time of King Edward (*tempore regis Edwardi or T.R.E.*) in 1066, and "now," that is, in 1086. Population figures are usually given for 1086, and those are the only ones summarized here. The summary is complicated enough, but it is the result of certain simplifications and assumptions. Usually no distinction is made here among different classes of urban properties, even though there are significant differences between a house and a property which might contain more than one house. What the Domesday commissioners meant by a burgess can only be determined by a study of how they used the word. Villeins or villagers seem to have been of a higher status than bordars and cottagers, and slaves (*servi*) were at the very bottom. A place where burgesses lived might be called a borough (*burgus*), but it might also be called a city (*civitas*) or a town (*villa*); Stafford was called all three. And sometimes burgesses lived on a rural manor (*manerium*) little different from one occupied only by peasants. A few places were qualified as small (*parvus*) or new (*novus*).[1] A locality is included in this list if it was either called a borough or a city or said to have a burgess population, or paid one third of the revenues of its court to the local earl (earl's third penny), an obligation some scholars think shows burghal status. By a strict application of this rule, Bury St. Edmunds should be excluded, but the reader may consult the complete entry and make his own decision. Places are listed in the order in which they appear in the manuscript.

[1] On new boroughs see Stephenson, p. 30.

The statistics and estimates given here are based where possible on H. C. Darby et al., *The Domesday Geography of England,* 5 vols. (Cambridge, England, 1954–1967). Estimates marked with an asterisk are my own. The maps are from the volume on southwest England, pp. 231, 353. Reprinted by permission of Cambridge University Press. Passages of Domesday Book on Chester and Rhuddlan are from James Tait, *The Domesday Survey of Cheshire* (Manchester, 1916), pp. 79–87 and 238–241. Reprinted by permission of Manchester University Press. Those on Lincoln and Stamford are from C. W. Forster and Thomas Longley, *The Lincolnshire Domesday and the Lindsey Survey* (Lincoln, 1924), pp. 3 and 9. Reprinted by permission of the Lincoln Record Society. The Domesday records of most other counties have been translated in the *Victoria County History,* which has been consulted for the other passages.

As was explained earlier,[2] Domesday Book records a number of properties or burgesses at a given borough but attached or appurtenant to a rural manor, and sometimes, as indicated in this summary, these are the only references we have to the population of the borough. For purposes of estimating population, I have treated all appurtenant burgesses as residents of their boroughs, even though some of them may have spent at least part of the year on their manors. Maps of the manors appurtenant to Oxford and Winchester are included here.

Domesday Book is a mine of information on all sorts of topics, as some of the following extracts show. It is also a very frustrating book, for by telling us as much as it does about eleventh-century England, it reminds us constantly of how much we do not know.

Volume One

Kent

1. Dover (*villa*): No record. No estimate possible.
2. Canterbury (*civitas*): 438 burgesses; 161 properties. Estimated population about 2,500.
3. Rochester (*civitas*): 5 burgesses; 113 properties. Estimated population 500, but possibly considerably more.
4. Sandwich (*burgus*): 415 properties. Estimated population about 2,000.
5. Fordwich (*parvus burgus*): 6 burgesses; 80 properties. Estimated population at least 400 or so.
6. Seasalter (*parvus burgus*): 48 bordars. Estimated population about 250.*
7. Hythe (*burgus*): No main entry. 231 appurtenant burgesses. Estimated population over 1,000.
8. Romney (*burgus*): No main entry. 156 appurtenant burgesses. Estimated population at least 800.

Sussex

9. Rye (*novus burgus*): 64 burgesses; 103 villeins; 4 cottagers. Estimated population at least 300, possibly considerably more.
10. Steyning (*burgus*): 223 villeins; 96 bordars; 9 slaves; 123 properties. Estimated population at least 600, possibly much more.
11. Pevensey: 110 burgesses, 1 property. Estimated population over 500.
12. Chichester (*civitas*): 9 burgesses; 292½ properties; 3 crofts. Estimated population 1,200–1,500.
13. Arundel (*burgus*): 4 burgesses; 13 properties. No estimate possible.
14. Lewes (*burgus*): 180 burgesses; 258 properties. Estimated population about 2,000.
15. Hastings: No main entry. 14 bordars; 24 appurtenant burgesses. No estimate possible.

Surrey

16. Guildford (*villa*): 75 haws wherein live 175 men; 6 other properties. Estimated population about 750.
17. Southwark: 1 bordar; many appurtenant burgesses; 47 properties. No estimate possible.

Hampshire

18. Winchester (*civitas*): No main entry. 114 appurtenant properties (see map; p. 75). No estimate possible.
19. Twynham (*burgus*): 32 villeins; 18 bordars; 4 radmen;[3] 3 freedmen; 3 slaves; 39 properties. Estimated population about 500.
20. Southampton (*burgus*): 79 men; 65 Frenchmen; 31 Englishmen; 55 (?) properties. Estimated population at least 1,200, perhaps much more.

Berkshire

21. Wallingford (*burgus*): Somewhere between 517 and 555 properties. Estimated population 2,000–3,000.

[2] See above, pp. 23–25.

[3] A radman was a tenant who performed service on horseback.

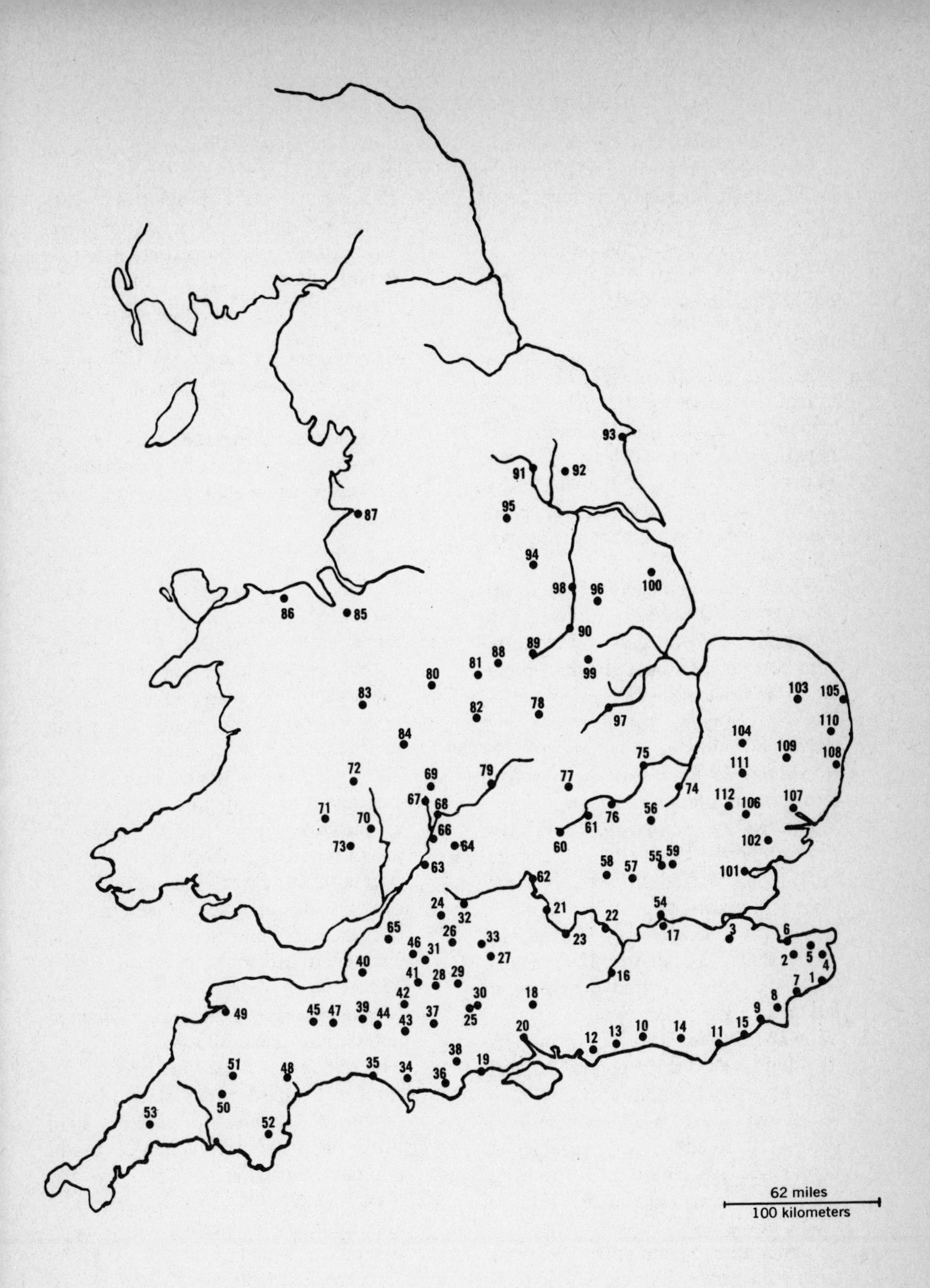

DOMESDAY BOROUGHS, 1086

22. [OLD] WINDSOR (*villa*): 22 villeins; 2 bordars; 1 priest; 1 slave; 95 properties. Estimated population about 500.
23. READING (*burgus*): 64 villeins; 38 bordars; 59 properties. Estimated population at least 650.

Wiltshire

24. MALMESBURY (*burgus*): 11 appurtenant burgesses; 80¾ properties; 9 cottagers outside the borough. Estimated population at least 400–500.
25. WILTON (*burgus*): No main entry. 25 appurtenant burgesses; 5 appurtenant properties. No estimate possible.
26. CALNE (*villa, manerium*): 14 slaves; 44 villeins; 80 bordars; 10 freedmen; 11 cottagers; 73 burgesses; 1 appurtenant property. Estimated urban population at least 300–400.
27. BEDWYN (*villa, manerium*): 18 slaves; 80 villeins; 60 cottagers; 14 freedmen; 25 burgesses. No estimate of urban population possible.
28. WARMINSTER (*manerium*): 24 slaves; 13 swineherds; 15 villeins; 8 cottagers; 14 freedmen; 30 burgesses. No estimate of urban population possible.
29. TILSHEAD (*manerium*): 22 slaves; 10 freedmen; 34 villeins; 32 cottagers; 66 burgesses. Estimated urban population at least 300.
30. SALISBURY (*manerium*): 67 bordars; 31 villeins. Paid third penny. No estimate of urban population possible.
31. BRADFORD-ON-AVON (*manerium*): 9 slaves; 18 freedmen; 36 villeins; 40 bordars; 22 swineherds; 33 burgesses; 1 servant. No estimate of urban population possible.
32. CRICKLADE: No main entry. 33 appurtenant burgesses; 2 appurtenant properties. No estimate possible.
33. MARLEBOROUGH: No main entry. Paid third penny. No estimate possible.

Dorsetshire

34. DORCHESTER: 89 properties; 1 appurtenant burgess. Estimated population nearly 700.
35. BRIDPORT: 100 properties. Estimated population about 500 or more.
36. WAREHAM: 135 properties; 4 appurtenant burgesses; 7 appurtenant houses. Estimated population at least 700.
37. SHAFTSBURY (*burgus*): 177 properties. Estimated population at least 1,000.
38. WIMBORNE MINSTER: 14 appurtenant properties; 8 appurtenant burgesses. Estimated population over 400.

Somersetshire

39. LANGPORT (*burgus*): 39 burgesses. Estimated population about 200.
40. AXBRIDGE (*manerium*): 32 burgesses. Estimated population about 160.
41. FROME: 6 freedmen; 36 bordars; 31 villeins. Paid third penny. No estimate of urban population possible.
42. BRUTON (*manerium*): 5 slaves; 4 freedmen; 28 villeins; 29 bordars; 17 burgesses; 1 swineherd. Estimated urban population about 85.
43. MILBOURNE PORT (*manerium*): 9 slaves; 20 bordars; 70 villeins; 67 burgesses; 2 appurtenant properties. Estimated urban population about 350.
44. ILCHESTER: 108 burgesses. Estimated population about 500.
45. MILVERTON (*burgus* in Exeter version of Domesday): 3 slaves; 3 cottagers; 3 bordars; 16 villeins. Paid third penny. No estimate of urban population possible.
46. BATH (*burgus*): 192 burgesses; 7 appurtenant properties. Estimated population about 1,000.
47. TAUNTON: 8 villeins; 82 bordars; 70 slaves; 16 freedmen; 17 swineherds; 64 burgesses. Estimated urban population over 300.

Devonshire

48. EXETER (*civitas*): 398 properties. Estimated population about 2,000.

49. BARNSTAPLE (*burgus*): 40 burgesses within the borough and 9 without; 18 other burgesses; 2 properties. Estimated population about 350.
50. LYDFORD (*burgus*): 28 burgesses within the borough and 41 without. Estimated population about 350.
51. OKEHAMPTON (*manerium*): 31 villeins; 11 bordars; 18 slaves; 6 swineherds; 4 burgesses at the castle. No estimate of urban population possible.
52. TOTNES (*villa*): 95 burgesses within the borough; 15 without the borough who work the land; 1 appurtenant burgess. Estimated population about 550.

Cornwall

53. BODMIN: 6 bordars; 5 villeins; 68 properties. Estimated population at least 400.

Middlesex

54. LONDON: No main entry. Over 78 appurtenant burgesses and 106 properties attached to places in Surrey, Middlesex and Essex. No estimate possible.

Hertfordshire

55. HERTFORD (*burgus*): 18 burgesses; possibly other burgesses; 36 properties. Estimated population 250–1,000.
56. ASHWELL (*manerium*): 14 burgesses; 24 villeins; 19 bordars; 17 cottagers; 8 slaves; 1 priest. Estimated population 400–500.
57. ST. ALBANS (*villa*): 46 burgesses; 4 Frenchmen; 16 villeins; 13 bordars; 12 cottagers. Estimated population 500 or more.
58. BERKHAMSTEAD (*villa, manerium*): 52 burgesses; 14 villeins; 15 bordars; 6 slaves; 1 priest; 1 ditcher. Estimated population at least 500.
59. STANSTEAD ABBOTS (*manerium*): 7 burgesses; 4 Frenchmen; 1 sokeman;[4] 4 villeins; 4 bordars; 7 cottagers; 2 slaves; 1 reeve; 1 priest. Estimated population under 200.

Buckinghamshire

60. BUCKINGHAM, with Bourton (*burgus*): 26 burgesses; 27 other burgesses (?); 3 villeins; 14 bordars; 10 cottagers; 2 slaves. No estimate possible; apparently a primitive agricultural community.
61. NEWPORT PAGNELL (*manerium*): Unspecified number of burgesses; "other men" and "men who dwell in the wood"; 5 villeins; 9 slaves. No estimate possible.

Oxfordshire

62. OXFORD (*civitas, villa*): Possibly as many as 1,070 properties (including 593 waste houses and 15 that paid nothing). Certainly 938 properties (see map for appurtenant burgesses). Estimated population 4,000–5,000.

Gloucestershire

63. GLOUCESTER (*civitas*): 24 properties; 81 appurtenant burgesses. No estimate possible.
64. WINCHCOMBE (*burgus*): 32 appurtenant burgesses. No estimate possible.
65. BRISTOL, attached to manor of Barton: Unspecified number of burgesses; 12 appurtenant properties. No estimate possible.
66. TEWKESBURY (*manerium*): 13 burgesses; 16 bordars; 72 slaves and bondwomen (presumably 36 male slaves). Estimated population at least 300, probably very much larger.

Worcestershire

67. WORCESTER (*civitas*): 7 appurtenant burgesses; 126 appurtenant properties. No estimate possible.
68. PERSHORE (*manerium*): 28 burgesses, plus other confused references. No estimate possible.
69. DROITWICH: 115 burgesses; 4 salt workers; 7 villeins; 35 properties. Estimated population 800 or more.*

[4] A sokeman was a tenant who owed service at his lord's court.

Herefordshire

70. HEREFORD (*civitas*): Only fragmentary figures (228 burgesses in 1066). No estimate possible.
71. CLIFFORD (*burgus, castellum*): 16 burgesses; 13 bordars; 4 oxmen; 5 Welshmen; 6 slaves; 4 bondwomen. Estimated population about 200.*
72. WIGMORE (*burgus*): 4 slaves only recorded population. No estimate possible.
73. EWIAS HAROLD (*castellum*): 31 bordars; 1 priest; 4 oxmen; 1 man; 13 Welshmen; 3 slaves; 2 properties in the castle. Estimated population about 200.*

Cambridgeshire

74. CAMBRIDGE (*burgus*): 29 burgesses; 3 Frenchmen; 1 priest; 324 properties. Estimated population at least 1,600, probably more.

Huntingdonshire

75. HUNTINGDON (*burgus*): 256 burgesses; 100 bordars; 3 fishermen. Estimated population at least about 2,000.

Bedfordshire

76. BEDFORD (*villa*): Unspecified number of burgesses. No estimate possible.

Northamptonshire

77. NORTHAMPTON (*burgus*): 87 burgesses (including 40 "in the new borough"); 204 properties. Estimated population at least 1,500.

Leicestershire

78. LEICESTER (*civitas*): 65 burgesses; 3 villeins; 12 bordars; 1 priest; the "men" of countess Judith; 320 properties. Estimated population perhaps 2,000 or more.

Warwickshire

79. WARWICK (*burgus*): 22 burgesses; 248 properties. Estimated population at least 1,000.

Staffordshire

80. STAFFORD (*civitas, burgus, villa*): 36 burgesses; 13 villeins; 8 bordars; 4 slaves; 13 canons; 96 inhabited properties; 65 waste properties. Estimated population at least 750.
81. TUTBURY (*burgus circa castellum*): 42 men who devoted themselves wholly to trade. No estimate possible.
82. TAMWORTH: 22 apurtenant burgesses, including 8 who work at Drayton "like other villeins." No estimate possible.

Shropshire

83. SHREWSBURY (*civitas*): 151 burgesses (?); 40 appurtenant burgesses; plus an unknown number belonging to the abbey. Estimated population at least 1,000 and probably considerably more.
84. QUATFORD (*burgus*): No details given, but certainly very small.

Cheshire

85. CHESTER (*civitas*): 37 burgesses; 283 properties. Estimated population at least 1,500.
86. RHUDDLAN (*novus burgus*): 18 burgesses. No estimate possible.

Between Ribble and Mersey (Lancashire)

87. PENWORTHAM: 6 burgesses; 3 radmen; 8 villeins; 4 oxmen. Estimated population about 100.*

Derbyshire

88. DERBY (*burgus*): 100 burgesses; 40 lesser burgesses; 16 properties; 103 waste properties. Estimated population at least 700.

Nottinghamshire

89. NOTTINGHAM (*burgus*): 120 men; 28 bordars; 11 villeins; 141 properties; 48 merchants' houses and 25 knights' houses. Estimated population 1,000–2,000 and perhaps more.
90. NEWARK, with two other places (*manerium*): 56 burgesses; 42 vil-

leins; 4 bordars; 8 priests; 7 freemen. No estimate possible.

Rutland

No Boroughs.

Yorkshire

91. York (*civitas*): 491 "inhabited" properties, great and small; 400 properties not "inhabited" but paying rent; 540 empty properties; 142½ other properties. Estimated population possibly between 4,000 and 5,000; possibly over 9,000 in 1066.
92. Pocklington (*manerium*): 15 burgesses; 13 villeins; 5 bordars; 4 rent-payers; 1 priest. Estimated population not more than about 200.
93. Bridlington (*manerium*): 4 burgesses. No estimate possible.
94. Dadsley, with two other places: 31 burgesses; 54 villeins; 12 bordars; 1 priest. Estimated population for 3 villages probably 400–500.
95. Tanshelf (*manerium*): 60 lesser burgesses; 16 villeins; 8 bordars; 16 cottagers; 1 priest. Estimated population 400–500.

Lincolnshire

96. Lincoln (*civitas*): 900 properties, together with 36 "outside the city." Estimated population 4,000–5,000 or more.
97. Stamford (*burgus*): About 494 properties. Estimated population 2,000–3,000 or more.
98. Torksey (*villa*): 102 burgesses. Estimated population 500 or so, probably more.
99. Grantham: 111 burgesses; "77 tofts of the sokemen of the thegns"; 72 bordars. Estimated population at least 1,200.
100. Louth (*manerium*): 80 burgesses; 40 sokemen; 2 villeins. Estimated population at least 600.

Volume Two

Essex

101. Maldon: 180 properties held by burgesses; 6 freemen; 1 sokeman; 9 villeins; 21 bordars; 5 slaves. Estimated population well over 1,100.
102. Colchester (*civitas*): 419 properties (burgesses?); 24 bordars; 2 villeins; 3 slaves. Estimated population well over 2,000 at an absolute minimum.

Norfolk

103. Norwich (*burgus*): 665 English burgesses; 480 bordars; (*novus burgus*): 36 burgesses; 6 Englishmen; 124 Frenchmen; 1 waste property. Estimated population 4,000–5,000 or more.
104. Thetford (*burgus*): 725 burgesses; 1 villein; 2 sokemen; 3 slaves; 30 bordars; 33 men. Estimated population at least 4,000, probably more.
105. Yarmouth: 70 burgesses; 24 fishermen. Estimated population at least 400, probably considerably more.

Suffolk

106. Sudbury: 118 burgesses; 2 villeins; 2 slaves. Estimated population up to 600 or more.
107. Ipswich (*burgus*): 110 burgesses; 100 poor burgesses; 12 freemen; 32 bordars; 8 villeins; possibly other burgesses. Estimated population at least about 1,300, probably very much more.
108. Dunwich (*manerium*): 236 burgesses; 2 bordars; 24 Frenchmen; 178 poor men; 80 men (?); 80 other burgesses (?). Estimated population about 3,000.
109. Eye (*manerium*): 25 burgesses; 9 freemen; 57 sokemen; 21 villeins; 32 bordars. Estimated population up to 700 or more.
110. Beccles: 26 burgesses; 12 freemen; 30 sokemen; 7 villeins; 46 bordars. Estimated population about 600, possibly more.
111. Bury St. Edmunds (*villa*): See

description on pp. 78–79. Estimated population possibly over 3,000.

112. CLARE (*manerium*): 43 burgesses; 5 sokemen; 30 villeins; 30 bordars; 20 slaves. Estimated population about 600 or more.

EXTRACTS FROM DOMESDAY BOOK

SEASALTER IN KENT

In the same district of Borowart a small borough named Seasalter which belongs to the archbishop's private kitchen. A certain person named Blize holds it of the monks. On the demesne is one plough-team, and [there are] 48 bordars with one plough-team. There [is] a church, and 8 fisheries with a rent of 25 *s.* Woodland [to render] 10 swine. *T.R.E.* and afterwards it was worth 25 *s.*, and now 100 *s.*

BACKWELL IN SOMERSETSHIRE

Fulcran and Nigel hold Backwell of the bishop. Turchil held [it] *T.R.E.* and paid geld for 10 hides. There is land for 14 ploughs. 32 villeins and 21 bordars and 2 slaves there have these [ploughs]. There is one burgess [*borgisū*] who lives at Bath and pays yearly 32 pence. There are 23 swine. There [is] a mill paying 4 *s.*, and 24 acres of meadow. Pasture 1 league long and half a league broad. Underbrush 1 league long and 2 furlongs broad. It was and is worth £8, and when received, it was worth as much.

ST. GERMANS IN CORNWALL

In this manor there was *T.R.E.* a market on Sundays, and now it is reduced to nothing by reason of the market which the count of Mortain has established hard by a certain castle of his, on the same day.

OXFORD IN OXFORDSHIRE

In the time of King Edward Oxford rendered yearly to the king for toll and rent and all other customary dues £20 and 6 measures of honey. And to Earl Algar £10 in addition to the mill which he had within the city. When the king went on an expedition 20 burgesses went with him for all the others or else they gave £20 to the king that all might be free.

Now Oxford renders £60 by count of 20 [pence] to the ounce. In this town [*villa*], as well within the wall as without, there are 243 houses which pay geld, and besides these there are 500 houses less 22 so waste and destroyed that they cannot pay geld.

The king has 20 mural dwellings which belonged to Earl Algar in King Edward's time, rendering then and now 14 *s.* less 2 pence, and he has one dwelling rendering 6 pence pertaining to Shipton-under-Wychwood and another rendering 4 pence pertaining to Bloxham and a third rendering 30 pence pertaining to Princess Risborough and two others rendering 4 pence pertaining to Twyford in Buckinghamshire. One of these is waste.

They are called mural dwellings for this reason, because if there be need and the king command it, they shall repair the wall.

[There follows a list of 29 holders of 217 dwellings.]

All the above-written hold these aforesaid dwellings free on account of the repair of the wall. All the dwellings which are called "mural" were free *T.R.E.* from every customary due except military service and the repair of the wall. . . . And if the wall is not repaired when there is need by him who ought, either he will pay 40 *s.* to the king or he loses his house. All the burgesses at Oxford have pasture in common within the wall which renders 6 *s.* and 8 pence.

BARTON IN GLOUCESTERSHIRE

This manor [of Barton] and Bristol [together] render to the king 110 marks of silver. The burgesses say that Bishop G[iso] has 33 marks of silver and one mark of gold besides the king's rent.

HEREFORD IN HEREFORDSHIRE

In the city of Hereford in the time of King Edward there were 103 men dwelling

10 miles
16.1 kilometers
Bloxham
Twyford
Whitehill
Bletchington
Hampton
Shipton under Wychwood
Taynton
Burford
OXFORD
Risborough
Steventon
Streatley
PLACES CONTRIBUTORY TO OXFORD
Faccombe
Stratfield
Eversley
Bramley
Basingstoke
Dummer
10 miles
16.1 kilometers
Clatford
Norton
Preston Candover
Nether Wallop
Houghton
Headbourne Worthy
Somborne
Mottisfont
WINCHESTER
Bramdean
Awbridge
West Meon
Romsey
Corhampton
Minstead
PLACES CONTRIBUTORY TO WINCHESTER

together within and without the wall, and they had the following customs:

If any one of them wished to withdraw from the city he could with the consent of the reeve sell his house to another man who was willing to do the service due therefrom, and the reeve had the third penny of this sale. But if anyone through his poverty could not perform his service, he surrendered his house without payment to the reeve, who saw that the house did not remain empty and that the king did not lack [his] service.

Within the wall of the city each whole burgage rendered 7½ pence and 4 pence for the hire of horses and on three days in August reaped at Marden, and [its tenant] was [present] on one day for gathering the hay where the sheriff pleased. He who had a horse proceeded three times a year with the sheriff to the pleas and to the hundred courts at Wormelow. When the king was pursuing the chase, from each house according to custom went one man to the beating in the wood.

Other men who had not whole burgages provided guards for the hall when the king was in the city.

When a burgess serving with a horse died, the king had his horse and weapons. From him who had no horse, if he died, the king had either 10 *s.* or his land with the houses [thereon]. If anyone, when he came by his death, had not bequeathed his possessions, the king had his goods. . . .

If the sheriff went into Wales with the army these men went with him. So that if anyone commanded to go did not go, he payed 40*s.* to the king as a fine.

In the same city Earl Harold had 27 burgesses who had the same customs as the other burgesses.

From the same city the reeve rendered £12 to the king and £6 to Earl Harold, and he had in his farm all the aforesaid customs.

The king, however, had in his demesne the three forfeitures, namely [for] breaking his peace, for attacking a house, and for assault.

Whosoever committed one of these [crimes], paid 100*s.* to the king as a fine no matter whose man he might be.

The king now has the city of Hereford in demesne, and the English burgesses dwelling there have their former customs; but the French burgesses are quit for 12 pence from all their forfeitures, except the three aforesaid.

CHESTER IN CHESHIRE

The city of Chester in King Edward's time paid geld for 50 hides. [There are] three hides and a half which are outside the city, that is, one hide and a half beyond the bridge and 2 hides in Newton and Redcliff and in the bishop's borough; these paid geld with the city.

There were in the said city *T.R.E.* 431 houses paying geld, and besides these, the bishop had 56 houses paying geld. This city then rendered 10½ marks of silver. Two parts went to the king and the third to the earl. And these laws obtained there:

1. If the peace given by the king with his [own] hand, by his writ or by his messenger, should have been broken by anyone, the king had thence 100*s.* But if the said peace of the king [were] given by the earl at his command [and] should have been broken, the earl had the third penny of the 100*s.* which were given for this [offence]. If, however, the same peace [were] given by the king's reeve or by the earl's servant [and] should have been broken, a fine of 40*s.* was paid, and the earl had the third penny.

2. If any free man, breaking the king's peace that had been given, should have killed a man in a house, all his land and chattels [*pecunia*] were the king's, and he became an outlaw. The earl had the same but only from his own man making this forfeiture. None, however, could restore peace to any outlaw, except through the king.

3. He who shed blood from the morning of Monday to noon on Saturday paid a fine of 10*s.* But from Saturday noon to the morning of Monday bloodshed incurred a

fine of 20*s*. Similarly, he paid 20*s*. who did this in the 12 days of the Nativity, and on Candlemas day, and on the first day of Easter and the first day of Whitsuntide, and on Ascension day, and on the day of the Assumption or of the Nativity of St. Mary, and on the day of the Feast of All Saints.

4. He who killed a man on these holy days paid a fine of £4, but on other days 40*s*. So, too, he who committed "hamfare" [attack on a house] or "forsteal" [assault] on these feast days and on Sunday paid £4; on other days 40*s*.

5. He who incurred "hengwite" [fine for a person who had been robbed and failed to raise the hue and cry] in the city paid 10*s*.; but a reeve of the king or earl, incurring this forfeiture, paid a fine of 20*s*.

6. He who was guilty of robbery or theft or did violence to a woman in a house paid for each of these a fine of 40*s*.

7. If a widow had unlawful intercourse with any man, she paid a fine of 20*s*.; but a maiden [paid] 10*s*. for the like offence.

8. Whoever in the city seized the land of another and could not prove it to be his paid a fine of 40*s*. Similarly, too, he who made claim thereto, if he could not prove that it ought to be his.

9. He who wished to take up his land or that of his kinsman gave 10*s*., and if he could not or would not, the reeve took his land into the king's hand.

10. He who did not pay his "gafol" at the term when it was due paid 10*s*. as a fine.

11. If fire burnt the city, the man whose house it came from paid a fine of 3 ounces of pence and to his next neighbor he gave 2*s*.

12. Two parts of all these forfeitures were the king's and the third [part] the earl's.

13. If ships arrived at or departed from the port of the city without the king's license, the king and the earl had 40*s*. from each man who was on the ships.

14. If a ship came against the king's peace and in spite of his prohibition, the king and the earl had both the ship and the men and all that was in it.

15. But if it should have come in the peace of the king and with his license, those who were on board sold what they had undisturbed. When it left, however, the king and the earl took 4 pence from each load. If the king's reeve ordered those who had marten pelts not to sell to anyone until they had first been shown to him and he had bought, whoever neglected this paid a fine of 40*s*.[1]

16. A man or woman caught giving false measure in the city paid a fine of 4*s*. Similarly, the maker of bad beer was either put in the cucking-stool or paid 4*s*. to the reeves. The officers of the king and earl took this forfeiture in the city in whosoever's land it arose, whether the bishop's or that of [any] other man. In like manner [they took] toll; whoever detained it beyond three nights paid a fine of 40*s*.

In this city there were *T.R.E.* 7 moneyers who, when the coinage was changed, paid £7 to the king and earl over and above the farm.

There were then 12 judges of the city and these were taken from the men of the king and the bishop and the earl. If any of them absented himself from the hundred [court] on the day of its session without sufficient excuse, he paid a fine of 10*s*. to the king and the earl.

For the repair of the city wall and bridge the reeve used to call up one man from each hide in the county. The lord of any man who failed to come paid a fine of 40*s*. to the king and the earl; this forfeiture was not included in the farm.

This city then rendered a farm of £45 and 3 "timbres" [probably a unit of 40 skins] of marten pelts. The third part was the earl's and two [parts] the king's.

When Earl Hugh received [it], it was not worth more than £30, for it was greatly wasted; there were 205 houses less than there had been *T.R.E.* There are now just the number he found [there].

Mundret held the city of the earl for £70

[1] Furs were a major item of trade with Ireland.

and one mark of gold. The same [Mundret] had at farm for £50 and 1 mark of gold all the earl's pleas in the county [court] and hundred [courts] except Englefield.

The land on which the church of St. Peter stands, which Robert of Rhuddlan claimed as thegn-land, never, as the county proved, belonged to a manor outside the city, but belongs to the borough and always paid dues to the king and earl like [the land] of other burgesses.

In Cheshire the bishop of the said city holds of the king what belongs to his bishopric.

Earl Hugh with his men holds of the king all the rest of the land of the county.

Roger the Poitevin held the land between Ribble and Mersey; the king holds [it] now.

The bishop of Chester has the following customary dues in the above-mentioned city:

1. If any free man works on a holy day, the bishop takes 8*s.* therefore; but for a slave [*servus*] or bondwoman breaking a holy day the bishop takes 4*s.*

2. If a merchant coming to the city with a bale of goods should break it open without the license of the bishop's officer between Saturday noon and Monday or on any other holy day, the bishop has for that offence 4*s.* as forfeiture.

3. If a man of the bishop find any man loading within the outer boundary of the city, the bishop takes therefor a forfeiture of 4*s.* or 2 oxen.

RHUDDLAN IN CHESHIRE

In this same manor of Rhuddlan a castle, likewise called Rhuddlan, has been lately made. There is a new borough and in it 18 burgesses [divided] between Earl [Hugh] and Robert. . . .

To these burgesses they granted the laws and customs which are [enjoyed] in Hereford and Breteuil, namely, that throughout the year they shall pay only 12 pence for any forfeiture, except homicide and theft and premeditated "hamfare" [assault on a house]. In the year of this inquest the toll of this borough was let to farm at 3*s.*

LINCOLN IN LINCOLNSHIRE

In the city of Lincoln there were *T.R.E.* 970 inhabited properties. This number is reckoned according to the English method, 100 counting for 120. In the same city there were 12 lawmen [*lagemanni*], that is [men] having sac and soc; — Hardecnut; Suartin, son of Grimbold; Ulf, son of Suertebrand, who had toll and team; Walraven; Alwold; Britric; Guret; Ulbert; Godric, son of Eddeve; Siward; Lewine; and Aldene.

Now there are as many there having sac and soc in like manner: Suardinc in the place of his father Hardecnut; Suartinc; Sortebrand in the place of his father Ulf; Agemund in the place of his father Walraven; Alwold; Godwin, son of Brictric; Norman Crassus in the place of Guret; Ulbert, brother of Ulf, who is still living; Peter of Volognes in the place of Godric, son of Eddeve; Ulnod the priest in the place of Siward the priest; Buruolt in the place of his father who is now a monk; Ledwine, son of Ravene, in the place of Aldene the priest.

STAMFORD IN LINCOLNSHIRE

In Stamford there were *T.R.E.* 12 lawmen [*lagemanni*] who used to have sac and soc within their own houses and over their own men, excepting geld and heriot, and forfeiture of their bodies up to 40 ores of silver, and excepting larceny. The same have this now, but there are only nine [of them].

BURY ST. EDMUNDS IN SUFFOLK

In the town [*villa*] where rests enshrined Saint Edmund, king and martyr, of glorious memory, Abbot B[aldwin] held *T.R.E.*, towards the provision of the monks, 118 men; and they could give or sell their land; and under them 52 bordars from whom the abbot can have some little aid, 54 freemen quite poor, 43 almsmen, each of them has one bordar. Now [there are] 2 mills and 2 stews or fishponds. This town was then worth £10, now £20. It is 1½ leagues in length and as much in breadth. And when a pound is levied on the hundred for geld, then there go from the town 60 pence towards the sustenance of the monks. But this refers to the town as [it was] *T.R.E.* as if [it were still] so; for now the town is contained in a greater circle, including land which then used to be ploughed and sown, whereon there are 30 priests, deacons and clerks together; 28 nuns and poor persons who daily utter prayers for the king and for all Christian people; 80 less 5 bakers, ale-brewers, tailors, washerwomen, shoemakers, robemakers, cooks, porters, agents together. And all these daily wait upon the Saint, the abbot and the brethern. Besides whom there are 13 reeves over the land who have their houses in the said town, and under them 5 bordars. Now 34 knights, French and English together, and under them 22 bordars. Now altogether [there are] 342 houses on the demesne of the land of Saint Edmund which was under the plough *T.R.E.*

Town Charters

A charter of privileges put a town's freedoms on record, and without one a town might have a difficult time proving that it had held customary rights since time immemorial. The existence of a charter is therefore some measure of a town's status and also, since charters were usually purchased, of its economic vitality. The privileges held by chartered towns varied greatly, however, and some towns of importance received charters late in the medieval period or not at all. As time passed towns attempted to acquire more and more privileges in charters which became increasingly specific. The contrast between two charters for Bristol is shown here, though not the difference between the charter of Henry I for London and that first granted to the city by William the Conqueror. Note that in 1299 Kingston-on-Hull did not receive all the privileges held by the citizens of London in 1133. The list at the end of the selection gives the date of the earliest known charter of boroughs which received grants before the death of England's greatest seller of charters, King John. Information on a few other towns chartered after 1216 has also been included. Towns created by or for a mesne lord (a vassal of the king) or held by someone other than the king or queen before 1066 have been marked by an asterisk. Among other towns which were mediatized at one time or another were Bath, Leicester, Warwick, Reading, and Exeter.

Charter of Robert Fitz Haimo for Burford (1088–1107)

Robert, son of Haimo, to all his men and friends, greeting. . . . Further I grant that each of the [burgesses of Burford] shall be able to sell or place in pledge a house, land, or any property, and may make his heir his son, daughter or wife or any other person without asking permission of his lord. And let them have the gild

The first two selections are from *English Historical Documents*, vol. II, ed. David C. Douglas and George W. Greenaway (London, 1953), pp. 965 and 945. Reprinted by permission of Eyre & Spottiswoode Ltd. The third and fourth selections are from N. D. Harding, *Bristol Charters*, vol. I, (Bristol, 1930), pp. 2–3 and 8–13. Reprinted by permission of the Bristol Record Society. The last selection is from Public Record Office, Charter Roll C. 53/85, membrane 2 (no. 27). Translated by the editor. The list is based (with some emendations) upon *British Borough Charters*, vol. I, ed. A. Ballard (Cambridge, England, 1913).

and customs which the burgesses of Oxford have in the gild-merchant. And all those who wish to come to the market, may come and buy in the market whatever they wish, but not wool or hides unless they be men of the said town.

Charter of Henry I for London (1130–1133)

Henry, by the grace of God, king of the English, to the archbishop of Canterbury, and to the bishops and abbots, and earls and barons and justices and sheriffs, and to all his liegemen, both French and English, of the whole of England, greeting.

1. Know that I have granted to my citizens of London that they shall hold Middlesex at "farm" for 300 pounds "by tale" for themselves and their heirs from me and my heirs, so that the citizens shall appoint as sheriff from themselves whomsoever they may choose, and shall appoint from among themselves as justice whomsoever they choose to look after the pleas of my crown and the pleadings which arise in connection with them.[1]

2. No other shall be justice over the same men of London.

3. And the citizens shall not plead outside the walls of the city in respect of any plea; and they shall be quit of scot and of Danegeld and the murder-fine.

4. Nor shall any of them be compelled to offer trial by battle.

5. And if any one of the citizens shall be impleaded in respect of the pleas of the crown, let him prove himself to be a man of London by an oath which shall be judged in the city.

6. Let no one be billeted within the walls of the city, either of my household, or by the force of anyone else.

7. And let all the men of London and their property be quit and free from toll and passage and lestage and from all other customs throughout all England and at the seaports.

8. And let the churches and barons and citizens hold and have well and in peace their sokes, with all their customs, so that those who dwell in these sokes shall pay no customs except to him who possesses the soke, or to the steward whom he has placed there.

9. And a man of London shall not be fined at mercy except according to his "were," that is to say up to 100s.;[2] this applies to an offence which can be punished by a fine.

10. And there shall no longer be "miskenning" in the hustings court, nor in the folk-moot, nor in other pleas within the city.[3]

11. And the hustings courts shall sit once a week, to wit, on Monday.

12. I will cause my citizens to have their lands and pledges and debts within the city and outside it.

13. And in respect of the lands about which they make claim to me, I will do them right according to the law of the city.

14. And if anyone has taken toll or custom from the citizens of London, then the citizens of London may take from the borough or village where toll or custom has been levied as much as the man of London gave for toll, and more also may be taken for a penalty.

15. And let all debtors to the citizens of London discharge their debts or prove in London that they do not own them; and if they refuse either to pay, or to come and make such proof, then the citizens to whom the debts are due may take pledges within the city either from the borough or from the village or from the county in which the debtor lives.

16. And the citizens shall have their hunting chases, as well and fully as had their predecessors, to wit, in Chiltern and Middlesex and Surrey. . . .

[1] In return for farming all their obligations for £300 in counted pennies, the citizens of London could choose their own officers.

[2] This was the amount to be paid to a man's relatives if he were killed.

[3] See below, p. 96, note 4.

Charter of Henry II for Bristol (1155)

Henry, King of England and Duke of Normandy and Aquitaine and Count of Anjou, to Archbishops, Bishops, Abbots, Earls, Barons, Justices, Sheriffs and all men of his land, greeting. Know ye that I have granted to my burgesses of Bristol that they shall be quit of toll and passage and all custom throughout all my land of England, Normandy and Wales, wheresoever they and their goods shall come. Wherefore I will and firmly command that they shall have all their liberties and quittances and free customs fully and honourably as my free and faithful men and they shall be quit of toll and passage and all other custom. And I forbid that anyone disturb them hereupon, contrary to this my charter, upon forfeiture of £10. Witnesses. . . .

Charter of John, Count of Mortain, for Bristol (ca. 1189)

John, Count of Mortain, to all men and to his friends, French and English, Welsh and Irish, present and to come, greeting. Know ye that I have granted and by this present charter have confirmed to my burgesses of Bristol dwelling within the walls and without the walls up to the boundaries of the town, to wit, between Sandbrook and Bewell and Brightneebridge and the spring in the way near Aldebury by Knowle, all their liberties and free customs, as well, freely and entirely, or more so, as ever they had them in my time or in the time of my predecessors. Now the liberties which have been granted to them are these, to wit:

1. That no burgess of Bristol shall plead without the walls of the town concerning any plea except pleas of exterior tenements which do not pertain to the hundred of the town.

2. And that they shall be quit of the murder-fine within the boundaries of the town.

3. And that no burgess shall wage trial by battle except he have been appealed concerning the death of a foreign man who has been killed in the town and who was not of the town.

4. And that no one shall take a dwelling within the walls by assize or by livery of the marshals against the will of the burgesses.

5. And that they shall be quit of toll and lastage and passage and pontage and of all other customs throughout all my land and power.

6. And that none shall be adjudged to be in mercy as to his money except according to the law of the hundred, to wit, by forfeiture of forty shillings.

7. And that the hundred [court] shall be held only once in the week.

8. And that in no plea shall any be able to sue by miskenning.

9. And that they shall have justly their lands and tenures and their pledges and debts throughout all my land whosoever shall owe to them.

10. And that concerning lands and tenures which are within the town, right shall be done to them according to the custom of the town.

11. And that concerning debts which have been contracted in Bristol and concerning pledges made in the same place pleas shall be held in the town, according to the custom of the town.

12. And that if anyone anywhere in my land shall take toll of the men of Bristol, if he have not restored it after he shall have been required to restore [it], the reeve of Bristol shall take thereupon a distress at Bristol and shall distrain to restore [it].

13. And that no merchant from outside the town shall buy within the town of any outside man hides or corn or wool except of the burgesses.

14. And that no stranger shall have a tavern except in a ship, nor shall he sell cloths for cutting except in the fair.

15. And that no stranger shall tarry in the town with his wares in order to sell his wares except for forty days.

16. And that no burgess anywhere in my land or power shall be attached or dis-

BRISTOL

Key:

1 *original borough*
2 *11th-century addition*
3 *12th-century suburb*
4 *13th-century addition*
5 *Suburb beyond castle*

A to B *Old channel of River Frome*
A to C *New channel of River Frome (1240)*
Name *Bounds given in John's Charter (1188)*

From Carl Stephenson, *Borough and Town* (Cambridge, Mass., 1933), plate VIII. By permission of the Mediaeval Academy of America.

trained for any debt except he be debtor or pledge.

17. And that they shall be able to marry themselves and to give their sons and daughters and widows in marriage without license of their lords.

18. And that none of their lords on account of lands outside the borough shall have custody or gift of their sons or daughters or widows, but only custody of their tenements which are of their fee until they shall be of age.

19. And that there shall be no recognition [inquest by jury] in the town.

20. And that none shall take tine [a requisition of ale] in the town except for the use of the lord count, and that according to the custom of the town.

21. And that they shall be able to grind their corn wheresoever they will.

22. And that they shall have all their reasonable gilds as well as, or better than, they had them in the time of Robert and William his son, Earls of Gloucester.

23. And that no burgess shall be compelled to redemn anyone except he himself will, even though he be dwelling upon his land.

24. I have granted also to them all their tenures within the walls and without the walls up to the aforesaid boundaries in messuages, in gardens, in edifices upon the water and elsewhere wheresoever they be in the town to hold in free burgage, to wit: — by service of landgable which they render within the walls.

25. I have granted also that everyone of them shall be able to make improvement as much as he be able in making edifices everywhere upon the bank and elsewhere without damage to the borough and town.

26. And that they shall have and possess all lands and void places which are contained within the aforesaid boundaries to be built on at their will.

Wherefore, I will and firmly command that my aforesaid burgesses of Bristol and their heirs shall have and shall hold all their aforesaid liberties and free customs as is above written of me and my heirs as well and entirely, or more so, as ever they had them at what time they have been effectual, well and in peace and honorably without all impediment or molestation which any one shall do to them thereupon. . . . At Bristol.

Charter of Edward I for Kingston-on-Hull (1299)

E[dward, by the grace of God, King of England, Lord of Ireland and Duke of Aquitaine, to his] archbishops, [bishops, abbots, priors, counts, barons, justiciars, viscounts, reeves, servants, and all his bailiffs and faithful men,] greeting. Know ye that for the improvement of my town (*villa*) of Kingston-on-Hull and for the advantage and convenience of my men of the same town, we will and grant, for ourselves and for my heirs:

1. That my said town shall henceforth be a free borough (*liber burgus*), and the men of the same town shall be free burgesses and shall have forever all the liberties and free customs pertaining to a free borough, provided that the borough shall be kept by some faithful man, chosen successively by us and my heirs for this purpose, who shall first take his corporal oath to the said burgesses on the holy gospels of God that he will preserve unimpaired all the liberties conceded by us to the burgesses and the borough, and will faithfully and diligently do all those things pertaining to the office of warden in the said borough.

2. We also grant for ourselves and for my heirs that the burgesses and their heirs and successors may bequeath in their last wills the lands and tenements which they have or shall henceforth have within the borough to whomsoever they will, freely and without any hindrance on the part of myself or my heirs or bailiffs whomsoever.

3. And that they shall have return of all of my writs in any way pertaining to the borough, so that no sheriff, bailiff or other servant of mine shall enter the borough to execute any duty there for any matter touching the borough, except in case of default of the warden of the town.

4. And that the burgesses shall not plead

or be impleaded anywhere but within the borough before the warden concerning any tenements within the borough, or transgressions committed or contracts made within the said borough.

5. And also that in pursuance of my writs from the chancery, the burgesses and their heirs shall choose a coroner out of their own number and shall present him to the warden, in whose presence he shall swear that he will faithfully perform and maintain those matters which pertain to the duty of a coroner in the borough.

6. And we also will and grant for ourselves and my heirs that there shall be one of my prisons in the borough for the punishment of malefactors apprehended there, and likewise a gallows shall be erected outside the borough on our soil, so that the warden shall be able to execute justice in cases of *infangenthef* and *outfangenthef* [thiefs caught inside and outside the limits].

7. We also will and grant for ourselves and my heirs that the burgesses and their heirs shall be forever quit of paying toll, pontage, passage, pavage, and murage and all other customs through all our kingdom and realm on their goods and wares.

8. And that all those of the borough who wish to enjoy the aforesaid liberties and free customs shall pay geld and scot with the burgesses whenever the borough is tallaged.

9. Also we grant to the burgesses for ourselves and my heirs that they and their heirs shall have forever two markets a week within the borough to be held in a place designated by us on Tuesdays and Fridays, and a yearly fair to be held for thirty days starting on the day of St. Augustine after Easter [May 26], unless the markets and fair shall be to the injury of neighboring markets and fairs. . . .

Given by our hand at Westminster on the first day of April [in the 27th year of our reign].

Borough Charters

Kent

1. Canterbury — 1103–04
2. Dover — 1154–89
3. Folkestone — 1135–41
4. Fordwich — 1077?
5. Hythe — 1156
6. Lydd — 1154–58
7. Rochester — 1154–89
8. Romney — 1154–89
9. Sandwich — 1077?

Sussex

10. Hastings — 1154–58
11. Lewes — 1148
12. Pevensey — 1207
13. Rye — 1140–89

Surrey

14. Guildford — 1130?
15. Richmond* — 1137–45

Hampshire

16. Andover — 1175
17. Chichester — 1135–54
18. Christchurch* (Twynham) — 1137–55
19. Petersfield* — 1183–97
20. Portsmouth — 1194
21. Southampton — 1154–66
22. Winchester — 1155–58

(Isle of Wight)

23. Newport* — 1177–84
24. Yarmouth* — *c.* 1170

Berkshire

Reading — 1253
25. Wallingford — 1156
Windsor (New) — 1277

Wiltshire

26. Cricklade — 1157
27. Devizes — 1135–54
28. Malmesbury — 1205–22
29. Marlborough — 1204
30. Salisbury
(Old Sarum) — 1200
(New Sarum*) — 1225
31. Wilton — 1121?

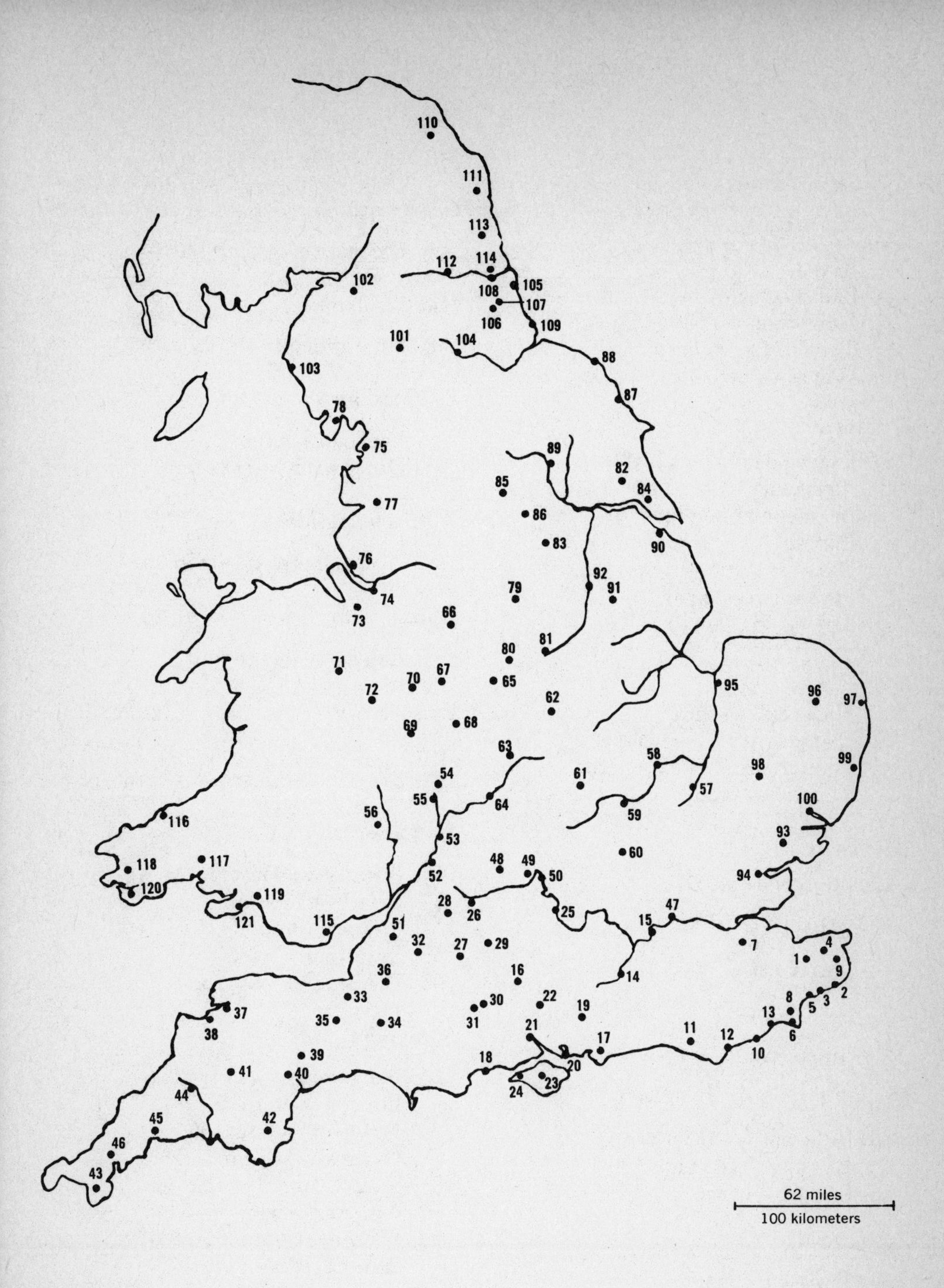

BOROUGHS CHARTERED BEFORE 1216

Dorsetshire

Bridport — 1253
Shaftesbury — 1252

Somersetshire

32. Bath — 1189
33. Bridgwater — 1200
34. Ilchester — 1204
35. Taunton — 1135–39
36. Wells — 1174–80

Devonshire

37. Barnstaple — 1154–58
38. Bideford* — 1204–17
39. Bradninch* — 1141–75
40. Exeter — 1154–58
41. Okehampton* — 1194–1242
    Plymouth — 1439
42. Totnes (?) — 1199–1216

Cornwall

43. Helston* — 1201
44. Launceston* — 1141–67?
45. Lostwithiel* — 1190–1200
46. Truro* — 1166

Middlesex

47. London — 1067?

Hertfordshire

Hertford — 1345

Buckinghamshire

Buckingham — 1554

Oxfordshire

48. Burford* — 1087–1107
49. Eynsham* — 1215
50. Oxford — 1156

Gloucester

51. Bristol — 1155
52. Gloucester — 1148
53. Tewkesbury — 1178–83

Worcestershire

54. Droitwich — 1215
55. Worcester — 1189

Herefordshire

56. Hereford — 1154–58

Cambridgeshire

57. Cambridge — 1120–31

Huntingdonshire

58. Huntingdon — 1113–22

Bedfordshire

59. Bedford — 1166
60. Dunstaple — 1131–33

Northamptonshire

61. Northampton — 1189

Leicestershire

62. Leicester — 1103–18

Warwickshire

63. Coventry* — *c.* 1153
64. Stratford-on-Avon* — 1196–98

Staffordshire

65. Burton-on-Trent* — 1197–1213
66. Leek* — 1209–28
    Lichfield — 1387
67. Stafford — 1206
68. Walsall* — *c.* 1200

Shropshire

69. Bridgnorth — 1157
    Ludlow — 1461
70. Newport — 1163–66
71. Oswestry* — 1190–1200
72. Shrewsbury — 1154–89
73. Chester — 1171
74. Frodsham* — 1209–28
    Rhuddlan* — 1278

Lancashire

75. Lancaster — 1193
76. Liverpool — 1207
77. Preston — 1179
78. Ulverston* — *c.* 1200

Derbyshire

79. CHESTERFIELD* — 1204
80. DERBY — 1204

Nottinghamshire

NEWARK — 1549
81. NOTTINGHAM — 1157

Yorkshire

82. BEVERLEY* — 1114–16
83. DONCASTER — 1194
84. HEDON — 1154–73
85. LEEDS* — 1208
86. PONTEFRACT* — 1194
87. SCARBOROUGH — 1155
88. WHITBY* — 1175–85
89. YORK — 1154–58

Lincolnshire

BOSTON — 1545
90. GRIMSBY — 1201
91. LINCOLN — 1154–58
STAMFORD — 1257
92. TORKSEY — 1154–76

Essex

93. COLCHESTER — c. 1130–33
94. MALDON — 1166–75

Norfolk

95. LYNN (KING'S)* — 1204
96. NORWICH — 1154–58
97. YARMOUTH — 1208

Suffolk

98. BURY ST. EDMUNDS* — 1102–03
99. DUNWICH — 1200
100. IPSWICH — 1200

Westmorland

101. APPLEBY — 1181

Cumberland

102. CARLISLE — 1154–89
103. EGREMONT* — c. 1202

Durham

104. BARNARD CASTLE* — c. 1175
105. BISHOP WEARMOUTH* — 1180–83
106. DURHAM* — 1154–81
107. ELVET* — 1189–1212
108. GATESHEAD — 1154–95
109. HARTLEPOOL* — 1201
110. NORHAM* — 1154–95

Northumberland

111. ALNWICK* — 1157–85
112. CORBRIDGE — 1201
113. MORPETH* —1188–1239
114. NEWCASTLE-ON-TYNE — 1154–89

Wales

115. CARDIFF* — 1147–83
116. CARDIGAN — 1199
117. CARMARTHEN — 1154–89
118. HAVERFORDWEST* — 1189–1219
119. NEATH* — 1147–73
120. PEMBROKE — 1154–89
121. SWANSEA* — 1153–84

Saints' Lives

Accounts of the lives of saints have value not only for religious history, but also as evidence about society and even economics. It is the life of St. Wulfstan, for instance, which records a major item of export to Ireland from late eleventh-century Bristol by reporting that the saint went to that port to preach against the slave trade. Pirenne, as we have seen, used the life of St. Godric before his conversion as his prototype of a parvenu merchant (p. 4). The life of St. Thomas of Canterbury by his secretary, William fitz Stephen, is unusual and especially valuable because William begins with a highly literary description of the city of London, the saint's birthplace. William, who wrote

From *English Historical Documents,* vol. II, ed. David C. Douglas and George W. Greenaway (London, 1953), pp. 956–961. Reprinted by permission of Eyre & Spottiswoode.

before 1183, is like many other authors of his time in embellishing his account with quotations from classical authors, some of whom he had read and others whom he knew only indirectly. The reader is warned that William's work is not free of exaggeration.

AMONG THE NOBLE and celebrated cities of the world that of London, the capital of the kingdom of the English, is one which extends its glory farther than all the others and sends its wealth and merchandise more widely into distant lands. Higher than all the rest does it lift its head. It is happy in the healthiness of its air; in its observance of Christian practice; in the strength of its fortifications; in its natural situation; in the honour of its citizens; and in the modesty of its matrons. It is cheerful in its sports, and the fruitful mother of noble men. Let us look into these things in turn. . . .

In the church of St. Paul there is the episcopal seat. . . . As regards the practice of Christian worship, there are in London and its suburbs 13 greater conventual churches and, besides these, 126 lesser parish churches.

It has on the east the Palatine castle,[1] very great and strong: the keep and walls rise from very deep foundations and are fixed with a mortar tempered by the blood of animals. On the west there are two castles very strongly fortified, and from these there runs a high and massive wall with seven double gates and with towers along the north at regular intervals. London was once also walled and turreted on the south, but the mighty Thames, so full of fish, has with the sea's ebb and flow washed against, loosened, and thrown down those walls in the course of time. Upstream to the west there is the royal palace[2] which is conspicuous above the river, a building incomparable in its ramparts and bulwarks. It is about two miles from the city and joined thereto by a populous suburb.

Everywhere outside the houses of those living in the suburbs, and adjacent to them, are the spacious and beautiful gardens of the citizens, and these are planted with trees. Also there are on the north side pastures and pleasant meadow lands through which flow streams wherein the turning of mill-wheels makes a cheerful sound. Very near lies a great forest with woodland pastures in which there are the lairs of wild animals: stags, fallow deer, wild boars and bulls. The tilled lands of the city are not of barren gravel, but fat Asian plains that yield luxuriant crops and fill the tillers' barns with the sheaves of Ceres.

There are also outside London on the north side excellent suburban wells with sweet, wholesome and clear water that flows rippling over the bright stones. Among those are Holywell, Clerkenwell and St. Clement's Well, which are all famous. These are frequented by great numbers and much visited by the students from the schools and by the young men of the city, when they go out for fresh air on summer evenings. Good indeed is this city when it has a good lord! [3]

The city is honored by her men, glorious in its arms, and so populous that during the terrible wars of King Stephen's reign the men going forth from it to battle were reckoned as 20,000 armed horsemen and 60,000 foot-soldiers, all equipped for war.[4] The citizens of London are regarded as conspicuous above all others for their polished manners, for their dress and for the good tables which they keep. The inhabitants of other towns are called citizens, but those of London are called barons. And with them a solemn pledge is sufficient to end every dispute.

The matrons of this city are very Sabines.

[1] The Tower of London.
[2] The Palace of Westminster.
[3] A jab at the king, Henry II. [Editor's note.]
[4] Compare this statement with the population figures given on pp. 67 and 104. [Editor's note.]

In London the three principal churches (that is to say, the episcopal church of St. Paul, the church of the Holy Trinity, and the church of St. Martin) have famous schools by special privilege and by virtue of their ancient dignity. But through the favour of some magnate, or through the presence of teachers who are notable or famous in philosophy, there are also other schools. . . .

Those engaged in business of various kinds, sellers of merchandise, hirers of labor, are distributed every morning into their several localities according to their trade. Besides, there is in London on the river bank among the wines for sale in ships and in the cellars of the vintners a public cook-shop. There daily you may find food according to the season, dishes of meat, roast, fried and boiled, large and small fish, coarser meats for the poor and more delicate for the rich, such as venison and big and small birds. . . .

Immediately outside one of the gates there is a field which is smooth[5] both in fact and in name. On every sixth day of the week, unless it be a major feast-day, there takes place there a famous exhibition of fine horses for sale. Earls, barons and knights, who are in the town, and many citizens come out to see or to buy. . . .

By themselves in another part of the field stand the goods of the countryfolk: implements of husbandry, swine with long flanks, cows with full udders, oxen of immense size, and woolly sheep. There also stand the mares fit for the plough, some big with foal, and others with brisk young colts closely following them.

To this city from every nation under heaven merchants delight to bring their trade by sea. The Arabian sends gold; the Sabaean spice and incense. The Scythian brings arms, and from the rich, fat lands of Babylon comes oil of palms. The Nile sends precious stones; the men of Norway and Russia, furs and sables; nor is China absent with purple silk. The Gauls come with their wines.

[5] Smithfield.

London, as historians have shown, is a much older city than Rome, for though it derives from the same Trojan ancestors, it was founded by Brutus before Rome was founded by Romulus and Remus. Wherefore they still have the same laws from their common origin. This city is like Rome divided into wards; it has annual sheriffs instead of consuls; it has its senatorial order and lower magistrates; it has drains and aqueducts in its streets; it has its appointed places for the hearing of cases deliberative, demonstrative and judicial; it has its several courts, and its separate assemblies on appointed days.

I do not think there is a city with a better record for church-going, doing honor to God's ordinances, keeping feast-days, giving alms and hospitality to strangers, confirming betrothals, contracting marriages, celebrating weddings, providing feasts, entertaining guests, and also, it may be added, in care for funerals and for the burial of the dead. The only plagues of London are the immoderate drinking of fools and the frequency of fires.

To this it may be added that almost all the bishops, abbots and magnates of England are in a sense citizens and freemen of London, having their own splendid town-houses. In them they live, and spend largely, when they are summoned to great councils by the king or by their metropolitan [bishop], or drawn thither by their private affairs.

We now come to speak of the sports of the city, for it is not fitting that a city should be merely useful and serious-minded, unless it be also pleasant and cheerful. . . . Instead of shows in the theater and stage-plays, London provides plays of a more sacred character, wherein are presented the miracles worked by saintly confessors or the sufferings which made illustrious the constancy of martyrs. Furthermore, every year on the day called Carnival — to begin with the sports of boys (for we were all boys once) — scholars from the different schools bring fighting-cocks to their masters, and the whole morning is set apart to watch their cocks do battle in the schools, for the boys are given a holiday that day. After dinner all the young men of the town go out into the fields in the suburbs to play ball. The scholars of the various schools have their own ball, and almost all the followers of each occupation have theirs also. . . .

Every Sunday in Lent after dinner a fresh swarm of young men goes forth into the fields on war-horses, steeds foremost in the contest, each of which is skilled and schooled to run in circles. From the gates there sallies forth a host of laymen, sons of the citizens, equipped with lances and shields, the younger ones with spears forked at the top, but with the steel point removed. They make a pretence at war, carry out field-exercises and indulge in mimic combats. Thither too come many courtiers, when the king is in town, and from the households of bishops, earls and barons come youths and adolescents, not yet girt with the belt of knighthood, for the pleasure of engaging in combat with one another. . . .

Many of the citizens take pleasure in sporting with birds of the air, with hawks, falcons and such-like, and with hounds that hunt their prey in the woods. The citizens have the rights of the chase in Middlesex, Hertfordshire, all the Chiltern country, and in Kent as far as the river Cray. . . .

Narrative Histories

The Deeds of Stephen, an anonymous history of the civil war of the reign of King Stephen written at the middle of the twelfth century, has been attributed to Bishop Robert of Bath. The author was favorable to the king and his wife, and shows his dislike for Stephen's opponent, Matilda, the daughter of Henry I and wife of the Count of Anjou. The second selection is from the *Chronicle* of Jocelin of Brakelond, a monk of Bury St. Edmunds, who wrote early in the thirteenth century about events at his abbey and of his abbot, Samson. Jocelin naturally enough supported the claims of his abbey. Both works remind us that an author writes with a purpose in mind, and that purpose is not necessarily to tell the truth. Narrative histories must be read with particular caution, but if carefully used they can provide information of a kind which can be learned from no other source.

The Deeds of Stephen

BRISTOL IS ALMOST the richest city of all in the country, receiving merchandise by sailing-ships from lands near and far. It lies in the most fertile part of England and is by its very situation the most strongly fortified of all its cities. For just like what we read about Brundisium it is a part of Gloucestershire that makes the city, narrowing like a tongue and extending a long way, with two rivers washing its sides and uniting in one broad stream lower down where the land ends.[1] There is also a strong and vigorous tide flooding in from the sea night and day; on both sides of the city it drives back the current of the rivers to produce a wide and

The first selection is from *Gesta Stephani,* translated by K. R. Potter (Edinburgh, 1955), pp. 37–39, 80–83. The last selection is from *The Chronicle of Jocelin of Brakelond,* translated by H. E. Butler (Edinburgh, 1949), pp. 75–77, 132–134. Reprinted by permission of Thomas Nelson & Sons.

[1] See the map on p. 82.

deep expanse of water, and while making a harbor quite suitable and perfectly safe for a thousand ships it hems in the entire circuit of the city so closely that the whole of it seems either swimming in the water or standing on the banks. However, on one side of it, where it is considered more exposed to a siege and more accessible, a castle rising on a vast mound, strengthened by wall and battlements, towers and divers engines, prevents an enemy's approach. Into this they [the followers of Robert, Earl of Gloucester] summoned a stream of horsemen and their dependents on foot, or to be more accurate a torrent of robbers and brigands, on so huge and extraordinary a scale that to those who beheld it, it seemed not only great and formidable but appalling and beyond belief. For they appeared from different countries and districts and went there in all the greater numbers and all the greater joy inasmuch as they were allowed, under a rich lord and from a very strongly fortified castle, to commit against the most fertile part of England whatever seemed most pleasing to their eyes. . . .

Six miles from Bristol there is a town where little springs through hidden conduits send up waters heated without human skill or ingenuity from deep in the bowels of the earth to a basin vaulted over with noble arches, creating in the middle of the town baths of agreeable warmth, wholesome and pleasant to look upon. The town is called Bath[2] from a word peculiar to the English language signifying washplace, for the reason that the sick are wont to gather there from all England to wash away their infirmities in the health-giving waters, and the whole to see the wondrous jets of hot water and bathe in them. This town then, because it was easy to fortify, the people of Bristol tried to add to their resources. They arrived there in column unexpectedly at early dawn. Having brought scaling-ladders with them and other devices for climbing a wall they withdrew into a valley and waited a little while until scouts had examined the site of the town and the best way of taking it and they could all rush it together with an impetuous onslaught. . . .

So when at last by receiving hostages and men's homage she [Matilda, wife of the Count of Anjou] had brought the greater part of the kingdom under her sway, and on this account, as has been said, was mightily puffed up and exalted in spirit, finally she came to London with a vast army at the request of the inhabitants, who met her with entreaties. And when the citizens thought they had attained to joyous days of peace and quietness and that the calamities of the kingdom had taken a turn for the better, she sent for the richest men and demanded from them a huge sum of money, not with unassuming gentleness, but with a voice of authority. They complained that they had lost their accustomed wealth owing to the strife in the kingdom, that they had spent a great deal to relieve the acute famine that threatened them, that they had always obeyed the king until they were brought to the extremity of want, and therefore they made humble and dutiful petition to her that she might take pity on their misfortune and their low estate, set a limit to the exaction of money from them, spare the harassed citizens, even for a little while, the burden of any extraordinary payment; later, when after the lulling of the disturbances of war throughout the kingdom peace returned with more security, they would aid her the more eagerly in proportion as their own wealth expanded. When the citizens expressed themselves in this way she, with a grim look, her forehead wrinkled into a frown, every trace of a woman's gentleness removed from her face, blazed into unbearable fury, saying that many times the people of London had made very large contributions to the king [Stephen], that they had lavished their wealth on strengthening him and weakening her, that they had long since con-

[2] See "The Ruin," above, pp. 46–48.

spired with her enemies for her hurt, and therefore it was not just to spare them in any respect or make the smallest deduction from the money demanded. On hearing this the citizens went away gloomily to their homes without gaining what they asked.

Just about this time too the queen [Matilda of Boulogne, Stephen's wife], a woman of subtlety and a man's resolution, sent envoys to the countess [Matilda] and made earnest entreaty for her husband's release from his filthy dungeon and the granting of his son's inheritance, though only that to which he was entitled by her father's will; but when she was abused in harsh and insulting language and both she and those who had come to ask on her behalf completely failed to gain their request, the queen, expecting to obtain by arms what she could not by supplication, brought a magnificent body of troops across in front of London from the other side of the river and gave orders that they should rage most furiously around the city with plunder and arson, violence and the sword, in sight of the countess and her men. The people of London then were in grievous trouble. On the one hand the country was being stripped before their eyes and reduced by the enemy's ravages to a habitation for the hedgehog, and there was no one ready to help them; on the other that new lady of theirs was going beyond the bounds of moderation and sorely oppressing them, nor did they hope that in time to come she would have bowels of mercy or compassion for them, seeing that at the very beginning of her reign she had no pity on her subjects and demanded what they could not bear. Therefore they judged it worthy of consideration to make a new pact of peace and alliance with the queen and join together with one mind to rescue their king and lord from his chains, since having incurred a just censure for too hastily and too heedlessly abandoning the king they were in some fashion accepting, while he was still alive, the tyranny of usurpers that was laid upon them.

So when the countess, confident of gaining her will, was waiting for the citizens' answer to her demand the whole city, with the bells ringing everywhere as a signal for battle, flew to arms, and all, with the common purpose of making a most savage attack on the countess and her men, unbarred the gates and came out in a body, like thronging swarms from beehives. She, with too much boldness and confidence, was just bent on reclining at a well-cooked feast, but on hearing the frightful noise from the city and getting secret warning from someone about the betrayal on foot against her she with all her retinue immediately sought safety in flight. They mounted swift horses and their flight had hardly taken them farther than the suburbs when, behold, a mob of citizens, great beyond expression or calculation, entered their abandoned lodgings and found and plundered everywhere all that had been left behind in the speed of their unpremeditated departure. Though a number of barons had fled with the countess under the stress of fear, she did not however keep them as permanent companions in this disorderly flight; they were so wonderfully shaken by the tumult of the sudden panic that they quite forgot about their lady and thought rather of saving themselves by making their own escape, and taking different turnings, the first that met them as they fled, they set off for their own lands by a multitude of byroads, as though the Londoners were hot on their heels.

The Chronicle of Jocelin of Brakelond

The merchants of London desired to be quit of toll at the market of St. Edmund; none the less many of them paid it, though unwillingly and under compulsion; and there was great disturbance and commotion concerning this among the citizens of London in the hustings court. Therefore they came and spoke to Abbot

Samson on the matter, saying that they had the right to be quit of toll throughout all England in virtue of the charter which they had from King Henry II.[1] To this the Abbot replied that, if it should be necessary, he might well call the King to warrant that he had never given them any charter to the prejudice of our Church nor to the detriment of the liberties of St. Edmund, to whom the holy Edward granted and confirmed toll and team [*i.e.,* the right to collect toll and hold court] and all royal rights before the Conquest of England; and that King Henry gave the citizens of London quittance from toll through his own dominions, where he could give it, but in the town of St. Edmund he could not give it, since it was not his to give. Hearing this, the citizens of London decreed by common consent that none of them should come to the market of St. Edmund, and for two years they absented themselves; from which our market suffered great loss, and the oblations received by the Sacrist were greatly diminished. At length, thanks to the intervention of the Bishop of London and many others, it was agreed between us and them that they should come to our market, and that some of them should pay toll, but that it should immediately be returned to them, in order that under this disguise the liberty of both parties should be preserved. But in process of time, after the Abbot had come to an agreement with his knights and, as it were, slept in peace, behold once more the cry arose, "The Philistines be upon thee, Samson!" For behold! the men of London threatened with one voice that they would raze to earth the stone houses which the Abbot had built that year, or else distrain a hundredfold upon the men of St. Edmund, unless the Abbot should speedily set right the wrong that had been inflicted upon them by the reeves of the town, who had taken fifteen pence from the carts of the citizens of London which had passed through the town carrying pickled herring from Yarmouth. And the citizens of London said that they had been quit of toll in every market at all times and places throughout all England, ever since the day when Rome first was founded; and that the city of London had been founded at the same time, and ought to have this liberty throughout all England, both because it was a privileged city, which had of old been the metropolitan city and capital of the realm and because it was of such ancient date.[2] But the Abbot asked for a suitable truce on this matter, until our lord the King should return to England, that he might consult him thereon; and, after taking counsel with men learned in the law, he replevined those fifteen pence to the claimants, the question of the rights of each party being reserved. . . .

In the same year [1201] the monks of Ely set up a market at Lakenheath,[3] having the King's assent and a charter to that effect. At first we dealt peaceably with our friends and neighbors, and after first sending letters to the Lord Bishop of Ely, we sent messengers to the Chapter of Ely, asking them to desist from their enterprise, and adding that, for the sake of peace and for the preservation of our mutual love, we would, in all friendship, pay them fifteen marks, which was the sum given by them to secure the King's charter. I will say no more than this; they refused to desist, and threatening words were bandied to and fro,

> and Roman spears menaced
> the spears of Rome. [Lucan, I.7]

But we secured a writ of recognition to decide whether that market had been set up to our prejudice and to the detriment of the market of St. Edmund. And oath being taken, it was declared that it was done to our detriment. This being re-

[1] See above, p. 80, article 14.

[2] See above, p. 89.

[3] Lakenheath is 15 miles north-west of Bury and 11 miles east of Ely. [Editor's note.]

ported to the King, he caused inquiry to be made by his registrar as to the nature of the charter that he had granted to the monks of Ely; and it was found that he had granted this charter on condition that it was not to the detriment of neighboring markets. The King then, on the promise of forty paltry marks, gave us his charter to the effect that no market should henceforth be held within the liberty of St. Edmund without the Abbot's assent: and he wrote to Geoffrey FitzPeter the Justiciar that the market of Lakenheath should be abolished, and the Justiciar wrote to the Sheriff of Suffolk to the same effect. But he, knowing that he could not enter the liberties of St. Edmund nor exercise any power therein, charged the Abbot by his writ that he should carry out the business according to the form of the King's command. The Provost of the hundred therefore, coming thither on the market day with freemen to bear him witness, publicly on the King's behalf forbade the market, showing the letters both of the King and the Sheriff; but being received with insult and injury, he retired, having accomplished nothing. The Abbot postponed the matter for a time, being then in London; but after consulting wise men on the matter, he ordered his bailiffs to take men of St. Edmund with horses and arms and to remove the market and carry off in chains such buyers and sellers as they could find. Now about midnight some six hundred well-armed men set out for Lakenheath. But since scouts gave warning of their approach, all those who were at the market ran this way and that, so that not one of them was to be found. Now the Prior of Ely, suspecting the coming of our men, had come that same night with his bailiffs to defend the buyers and sellers to the best of his power; but he refused to leave his house, and when our bailiffs demanded gage and pledge from him that he would stand to right in the court of St. Edmund in respect of the injury that he had done, and the Prior had refused his demand, then after taking counsel they overthrew the forked poles of the meat-market and the planks of the stalls in the market, and carried them off, and leading with them all the cattle, "all sheep and oxen, yea, and the beasts of the field," [Ps. 8:8] they proceeded towards Icklingham. The Prior's bailiffs followed them and demanded back their cattle, offering pledges for fifteen days; and it was done as they asked. Within fifteen days there came a writ summoning the Abbot to appear before the Exchequer to answer for what had been done, and ordering in the meantime that the captured beasts should be sent away in freedom. For the Bishop of Ely, an eloquent and fluent speaker, complained in person concerning this affair to the Justiciar and magnates of England, saying that an act of unprecedented arrogance had been committed on the land of St. Ethelreda in time of peace; and many others were stirred to indignation against the Abbot by his words.

Court Records

The records of court cases make a perfect complement to the laws themselves, for they show not what was supposed to happen, but what actually did. Pirenne postulated that merchants needed law which would be more expeditious and rational than that provided in the early middle ages, and that this need

The first selection is from *Select Cases Concerning the Law Merchant*, vol. I, ed. Charles Gross (London, 1908). Selden Society, vol. 23, pp. 3–6, 14, 20, 22, 36–37. The last selection is from Assize roll of 7 Edward I, *ibid.*, vol. III, ed. Hubert Hall (London, 1932). Selden Society, vol. 49, pp. 140–141. Reprinted by permission of the Selden Society.

was at the origin of the so-called "Piepowder" courts (p. 6). The rolls of one of these courts have survived, so that we know in considerable detail how justice was executed at the fair of St. Ives. In 1110 Henry I granted to the abbot of Ramsey the right to hold an annual fair at his village of St. Ives, on the river Ouse 6 miles east of Huntington, along with "soc and sac and infangenthef, just as any fair has in England." By the end of the thirteenth century the fair of St. Ives lasted from three to six weeks, and attracted merchants from many places on the continent, particularly from France and the Low Countries. It is noteworthy that while many could be found going to St. Ives, few stayed there; although the village had an enormous temporary population once a year, its international commerce never gave it the status or size of anything but a market town. The cases selected here give an indication of the speed of trial. While the court was conservative in using the old Anglo-Saxon legal forms of compurgation and miskenning (compare London, p. 80), it can be seen that a formal system which did not ask for evidence produced results based, at least at times, on negotiation, compromise and equity.

The second section is an extract from an assize roll relating a case which came before royal justices in 1279, when the men of Montgomery on the Welsh border complained that a market established by the lord of Welshpool was too close to their own market. The final settlement of the case is not known. Measured in modern statute miles, it is almost ten miles from Welshpool to Montgomery via Buttington bridge, and seven and a half by the most direct road.

Records of the Court of the Fair of St. Ives

Thursday, May 8, 1270

Peter Cousin of London complains of the community of Huy in a plea of debt; pledges to prosecute, Robert of Melbourn and Nicolas of Lyons. Of the said community of Huy John of Aust, Ansel of Pamel, and Roger Meuband are attached to answer by one piece of burnet,[1] and they have a day given them on the morrow to make concord.

William Motun of Sandwich complains of William de Hautemariage of Rom; pledges to prosecute, James of Bury St. Edmunds and William of Windsor; defendant's pledge, his goods which are attached by William of Graveley.[2] . . .

Friday, May 9, 1270

William de Hautemariage of Rom acknowledged that he owes William Motun of Sandwich 21*d*. Therefore by award of the court let him make satisfaction to William Motun for both the debt and 2*s*. damages, and he is in mercy 2*s*. [*i.e.*, a fine paid to the court] for the unjust detention; pledge, Robert Tailor. . . .

A love-day [*i.e.*, an opportunity for reconciliation] is given on the morrow to Peter Cousin of London plaintiff and to the community of Huy defendant, saving what should be saved.[3] . . .

Saturday, May 10, 1270

Peter Cousin plaintiff and John of Aust, Ansel of Pamel, and Roger Meuband of Huy defendants make concord; and the said John, Ansel, and Roger put themselves in mercy 6*s*. 8*d*. . . .

William of Eastnor has been attached by two pair of hose and two pair of shoes to answer John Currier of London and is not yet justiced. Therefore it is ordered that they be detained and more be taken. . . .

Tuesday, April 28, 1287

The jurors of the Green say that Ralph Keyse has received lepers in a certain

[1] Dark brown cloth of superior quality. [Editor's note.]

[2] A bailiff of the court. [Editor's note.]

[3] The saving clause means that even if the two parties agree to a settlement, the right of the court to a fine will not be lost. [Editor's note.]

house of his close to his neighbors and to the merchants to the great peril of his neighbors; fine 6*d*.

They say also that harlots are often received at night in the house of William Redknave; therefore he is in mercy; he is poor [*i.e.*, he cannot pay a fine]. . . .

Thursday, May 8, 1287

Robert of Langbaurgh complains of Henry of Bytham and says that on Tuesday last in front of the booths of the men of Brabant in the vill of St. Ives the said Henry maliciously assaulted him and threw him into a certain well and beat and maltreated him against the peace of the lord abbot to the damage of the said Robert a half-mark; and he produces suit. The said Henry is present and denies all, and is at his law [*i.e.*, he will swear his innocence with the support of oath-helpers], which he offers to make before his withdrawal from the court; whereupon one of his compurgators failed in making his law, because he named Robert when he should have named Henry. Therefore it is awarded that the said Robert be quit thereof,[4] and the said Henry is in mercy 6*d*. . . .

Friday, May 9, 1287

John, son of Alan of Colne, complains of Robert Marshal and his son Adam, and says that whereas on Wednesday last he brought a certain horse of his to the workshop of the said Robert and Adam to have three of the said horse's feet shod with new shoes and to have a fourth shoe removed for 2*d*., the said Robert and Adam removed the shoe from one foot of the said horse and put a new shoe on another foot, but they broke their covenant as to the other two feet; wherefore the said John by the delay of the said Robert and Adam lost the sale of his horse on that day from the third to the ninth hour to his damage a half mark. The said Robert and Adam are present and crave leave to make concord with John, and they make concord; and Robert and Adam put themselves in mercy 6*d*.; pledges, Martin Jamot and Robert Baldwin. . . .

Saturday, April 24, 1288

John, son of John of Eltisley, complains of Roger Barber, for that he has unjustly broken a covenant with him and unjustly because whereas the said John was in the vill of Ramsey on Monday [Jan. 13, 1287] after Epiphany last past, a year ago, in the house of Thomas Buck, the said Roger came there and undertook to cure his, John's, head of baldness for 9*d*., which the said John paid in advance; the next day, Tuesday, the said Roger put him in plaster and did likewise on Wednesday, and afterwards withdrew from the vill, so that from that day to this he would in no way interpose, to his, John's, damage a half-mark; and he produces suit. The said Roger was present and made denial, and put himself on his law, and in finding pledges of his law withdrew from the bar without leave. Therefore the said John craved judgment against him as against one who is convicted. Wherefore it is awarded that the said Roger make satisfaction to the said John for 9*d*., the sum claimed, and for his damages, which are remitted; and that he be in mercy 6*d*. for the trespass.

Assize Roll of 1279

And the aforesaid Griffin[5] comes and says that he ought not to have to reply to the aforesaid complaint of the men of Montgomery concerning his market or fair of Pool. For he says that the place is situate in the Welshry, and every lord

[4] If Henry had made his law, Robert would be in mercy for making a false claim. As it is, he receives nothing and pays nothing. This is an example of verbal error in making a formal oath, or "miskenning." [Editor's note.]

[5] Gruffydd ap Wenwynwyn, lord of Welshpool. [Editor's note.]

who has a town in the Welshry is licensed to set up a market and fair upon his land; for the setting up of which fair and market none can complain that it be to the harm of his fair or market if it be distant only from his fair and market as far as the town of Pool is distant from the town of Montgomery. And this he is prepared to aver according to the law of Wales. And he says that this is the law of Wales; and whereas the lord King granted to the Welsh that they ought to be dealt with according to the law of Wales, he says that he is not bound to answer the complaint of the men of Montgomery in any other manner.

And the aforesaid men of Montgomery come and say that the aforesaid Griffin, by grant of the lord Henry, father of the lord King, set up his market and fair, whereof he has a charter. And that, as is customary in such charters, the lord King granted to him a fair and market without harm to neighbouring fairs and markets. And yet they say that he first set up the fair and the market aforesaid by this charter. . . .

And the aforesaid men of Montgomery, questioned how far the town of Pool is distant from the town of Montgomery, so that [by travelling] with a horse and cart at any time of the year, they say that it is 4 miles distant [when the journey is made] by way of Baldwin's Bridge, which is now prostrated through the war and the violence of the Welsh. And this bridge the men of Montgomery say they are ready to repair.

And the aforesaid Griffin, asked how great the distance should be between the sites of fairs and markets according to the law of Wales, says that it suffices by that law that one should be distant from the other by the space of 4 miles. And he says that there are many markets in Wales where one is distant from another only three miles; and many which are distant from one another only two miles. He says also that the town of Pool is distant from Montgomery, going by Baldwin's Bridge, five miles, which bridge is utterly [broken asunder]; and by this there is no way for passage of carts in many parts in [*some seasons*] of the year, and then men go by way of Buttington Bridge; and by that road there are seven miles between the towns aforesaid.

And the aforesaid men of Montgomery say that the distance between the aforesaid towns is only 4 miles. Nor does proximity alone, as they say, suffice for the putting down of the fair and market aforesaid. They say also that a lord who holds his lands in chief of the lord King outside the county and in Welshry shall not set up a fair or market without the licence and grant of the lord King.

And because of the reasonings aforesaid a day is given to the parties before the lord King in one month from Easter Day.

Exchequer Records

The financial records of the English monarchy, going back to Domesday Book, are unparalleled in European archives. For the twelfth century, when we can only guess at the revenues of continental monarchs, we have roll after roll of original documents detailing the income of the English kings. One of these "Pipe Rolls" survives from the reign of Henry I (for 1130), and after 1156 the series is nearly unbroken. These documents tell us much about the financial obligations of the English towns, and thus about their comparative status and wealth. The annual payments in money or kind owed to the king from his domain, boroughs as well as royal manors, was known as his farm (for London see above, p. 80). The first part of the following table shows the amount in money recorded for the farm of each borough in royal hands in Domesday Book, and the size of the farm under Henry II and his son Richard, when that is known. Payments in kind have been omitted, with one exception, as have the distinction between payments in pure silver ("blanch"), weighed pennies, or counted pennies ("by tale"). The list is not exhaustive, since places like Bristol, which paid heavily as part of the manor of Barton in Domesday Book (p. 74), have been omitted, even though Bristol later rendered a separate farm. The second section records the "aids" (*auxilia* or *dona*) or extraordinary taxes which replaced the Danegeld and which were collected from the boroughs by Henry I and Henry II. The column for Henry I is based on his one surviving pipe roll; since that roll is incomplete the figures in brackets have been supplied from the earliest pipe roll of Henry II. Henry II's taxation of his boroughs was uneven. Figures are given here for the number of known aids collected from each borough, and their average size.

	BOROUGH FARMS (IN £)				AIDS (IN £)		
	1066	1086	*Henry II*	*Richard I*	*Henry I*	*No. of aids*	*Henry II (average)*
Kent							
CANTERBURY	51	54	49		20	7	41
DOVER	18	54	54	24			
ROCHESTER	5	40		25			
Sussex							
ARUNDEL	4	12					
CHICHESTER	15	35		39?		6	12
LEWES	26	34					
Surrey							
GUILDFORD	18	32			5	7	9
SOUTHWARK		16			5	7	8
Hants.							
SOUTHAMPTON	7?	7? + 4	300–200	107		4	22
WINCHESTER			143	143	80	7	81
Berks.							
NEWBURY			49				
READING		5					
WALLINGFORD	30	80	85–120	80	15	2	10
Wilts.							
BOROUGHS AS A GROUP					17		
CALNE						8	3
MALMESBURY	14	14					
MARLEBOROUGH						5	22
SALISBURY						6	5
WILTON		50				6	11
Dorset.							
BOROUGHS AS A GROUP					15		
SHAFTESBURY (ABBEY)		3					
Somerset.							
ILCHESTER		12	30	30		6	10
Devon.							
BARNSTAPLE		3					
EXETER		18		13	[20]	6	102
LYDFORD		3		4			
Middx.							
LONDON		300	522	300	120	6	665
Herts.							
BERKHAMSTEAD						4	43
HERTFORD	8	20	24		5	4	11

	BOROUGH FARMS (IN £)				AIDS (IN £)		
	1066	1086	*Henry II*	*Richard I*	*Henry I*	*No. of aids*	*Henry II (average)*
NEWPORT						5	11
Bucks.							
BUCKINGHAM	10	16					
Oxon.							
OXFORD	30	60			20	6	51
Gloucs.							
GLOUCESTER	36	60	50–55	55	15	7	60
WINCHCOMBE	6	28			3	4	2
Worcs.							
DROITWICH	74	65			[5]	2	17
WORCESTER	24	31	24	24	[15]	7	27
Herefords.							
HEREFORD	18	60	40	40	[10]	8	17
Cambs.							
CAMBRIDGE		14	60	60	12	6	35
Hunts.							
GODMANCHESTER						4	20
HUNTINGDON	45	45	20	45	8	5	18
Beds.							
BEDFORD		5	40	40	5	7	26
Northants.							
NORTHAMPTON		31	100–120	120	10	6	140
Leics.							
LEICESTER	30		75				
Staffs.							
NEWCASTLE						4	12
STAFFORD	9	7			3	7	14
TAMWORTH					3	6	4
Salop.							
BRIDGNORTH			5–7	7		7	8
NEWPORT						3	2
SHREWSBURY	30	40	20–27	27	[5]	7	28
Chest.							
CHESTER	45	70 plus 1 gold mark					
Derbys.							
DERBY	24	30		60	5[1]	6	14
Notts.							
NOTTINGHAM	18	30		52?	10[1]	4	27
Yorks							
DONCASTER						5	30
SCARBOROUGH			20–34	33		4	26

[1] Nottingham and Derby together rendered £15, here divided arbitrarily.

	BOROUGH FARMS (IN £)				AIDS (IN £)		
	1066	*1086*	*Henry II*	*Richard I*	*Henry I*	*No. of aids*	*Henry II (average)*
YORK	52	100		100	40	7	222
Lincs.							
GRIMSBY			111	111		4	31
HORNCASTLE						2	26
LINCOLN	30	100	180	180	60	8	164
STAMFORD	15	50			5		
TORKSEY	18	30					
Essex							
COLCHESTER	15	80	40	40	20	6	20
MALDON	13	16				5	7
Norf.							
CAISTER						4	22
NORWICH	30	90	108	108	30	8	176
THETFORD	30	76			10	7	12
YARMOUTH	27	28	40			6	11
Suff.							
DUNWICH	10	50 plus 60,000 herrings	120 plus 24,000 herrings	120 plus 24,000 herrings		4	125
IPSWICH	15	37		40	7	6	26
LOTHINGLAND						3	29
ORFORD			24–40			3	15
SUDBURY	18	28					
Northumb.							
CORBRIDGE						7	26
NEWCASTLE ON TYNE						7	31
Cumb.							
CARLISLE						5	26

Poll Taxes of 1377 and 1381

In 1377 the local officials of Edward III set out to collect a groat (a large silver coin worth 4 pence) from every man and woman over 14 in the kingdom, and four years later they collected another poll tax. The returns from 1377 give the most accurate basis we have for estimating the population of England before the first census in 1801. Adding in some 30,000 clergy who paid separately, making estimates for the counties palatine of Cheshire and Durham

Based upon Josiah C. Russell, *British Medieval Population* (Albuquerque, 1948), pp. 132–133, 141–143.

and for the genuine mendicants who were exempted from the tax, and calculating that approximately one third of the total population was under 14, the demographic historian Josiah Russell reaches a total figure for England in 1377 of over 2,200,000, double the Domesday population even after the terrible plagues during the third quarter of the fourteenth century. Plague hit urban centers harder than the countryside, which may explain why the percentage of people living in towns in 1377 was about the same or even less than it was in 1086. The tax collectors usually recorded the population of the boroughs separately from that of the shires, though the practice in 1377 and 1381 was inconsistent, and some places with large populations were buried in the shire returns. Chester and Durham, omitted from the survey, probably had populations of about 2,500 and 2,000 respectively. The following list gives the tax population of the shires and of all towns entered individually; towns with a tax population of over 800 which paid as part of the shire have been entered in brackets. These figures from 1377 should probably be increased by about 50% to estimate total population. The drastic drop between 1377 and 1381 was not the result of plague but rather suggests serious inefficiency and massive tax evasion.

	1377	*1381*
Bedfordshire	20,339	14,895
Berkshire	22,723	15,696
Bristol (*villa*)	6,345	5,662
Buckinghamshire	24,672	17,997
Cambridgeshire	27,350	24,324
Cambridge (*villa*)	1,902	1,739
Ely (*civitas*)	1,722	* * *
Cornwall	34,274	12,056
Cumberland	11,841	4,748
Carlisle (*civitas*)	678	* * *
Derbyshire	23,243	15,637
Derby (*villa*)	1,046	* * *
Devonshire	45,635	20,656
Exeter (*civitas*)	1,560	1,420
Plymouth (*villa*)	4,837	* * *
Dartmouth (*villa*)	506	* * *
Dorsetshire	33,251	19,507
Essex	47,962	30,748
Colchester (*villa*)	2,955	1,609
Gloucestershire	36,760	27,857
Gloucester (*villa*)	2,239	1,446
Hampshire	33,241	22,018
Isle of Wight	4,733	3,625
Southampton (*villa*)	1,152	1,051
Winchester (*civitas*)	1,440	* * *
Herefordshire	15,318	12,659
Hereford (*civitas*)	1,903	* * *
Ludlow (*villa*)	1,172	* * *
Hertfordshire	19,975	13,296
Huntingdonshire	14,169	11,299
Kent	56,557	43,838

LEADING TOWNS IN 1377

	1377	1381
Canterbury (*civitas*)	2,574	2,123
Rochester (*civitas*)	570	* * *
[Maidstone]	[844]	
Lancashire	23,880	8,371
Leicestershire	31,730	21,914
Leicester (*villa*)	2,101	1,708
Lincolnshire	87,461	59,764
Lincoln (*civitas* and *clausum*)	3,569	2,196
Stamford (*villa*)	1,218	* * *
Boston (*villa*)	2,871	* * *
Grimsby (*villa*)	* * *	562
London (*civitas*)	23,314	20,397
Middlesex	11,243	9,937
Norfolk	88,797	66,719
Norwich (*civitas*)	3,952	3,833
Lynn (*villa*)	3,127	1,824
Yarmouth (*villa*)	1,941	* * *
Northamptonshire	40,225	27,997
Northampton (*villa*)	1,477	1,518
Northumberland	14,162	return missing
Newcastle-on-Tyne (*villa*)	2,647	1,817
Nottinghamshire	26,260	17,442
Nottingham (*villa*)	1,447	1,266
Newark (*villa*)	1,178	* * *
Oxfordshire	24,982	20,588
Oxford (*villa*)	2,357	2,005
Rutland	5,994	5,593
Shropshire	23,574	13,041
Shrewsbury (*villa*)	2,082	1,618
Somerset	54,603	30,384
Bath (*civitas*)	570	297
Wells (*villa*)	901	487
[Bridgwater (*burgus*)]	[858]	
Staffordshire	21,465	15,993
Lichfield (*civitas*)	1,024	* * *
Suffolk	58,610	44,635
Ipswich (*villa*)	1,507	963
Bury St. Edmunds (*villa*)	2,445	1,334
Surrey	18,039	12,684
Southwark (*villa*)	* * *	1,059
Sussex	35,326	26,616
Chichester (*civitas*)	869	787
Warwickshire	25,448	20,481
Coventry (*villa*)	4,817	3,947
Westmorland	7,389	3,859
Wiltshire	42,599	30,627
Salisbury (*civitas*)	3,226	2,708
Worcestershire	14,542	12,043
Worcester (*civitas*)	1,557	932

	1377	1381
YORKSHIRE	119,572	63,903
YORK (*civitas*)	7,248	4,015
BEVERLEY (*villa*)	2,663	***
SCARBOROUGH (*villa*)	[1,393]	1,480
KINGSTON-ON-HULL (*villa*)	1,557	1,124
[PONTEFRACT]	[1,085]	
Totals	1,362,180	896,374

Epilogue

MAY McKISAK

IT HAS BEEN POSTULATED that after 1377 the urban populations, outside London, ceased to expand; and though this hypothesis may need some modification, it is undoubtedly true that not all the towns were prospering. Lincoln affords a melancholy example of a once noble city which in this century had fallen on evil days. She suffered badly from the Black Death, and the transfer of the wool staple to Boston in 1369 was significant of her general decline. Four years earlier Edward III had harshly informed the citizens that because of the uncleanliness of their streets, "the evil name of them and their city grows worse and worse"; they were said to be refusing to contribute to the cost of the new gildhall; and a former mayor and parliamentary representative was named among the insurgents of 1381. At the end of the century both Lincoln and Yarmouth complained that their inhabitants were departing because of inability to pay the farm. In his charter to Newcastle (1357) Edward III referred to the great impoverishment of the town; after a period of prosperity in the seventies, Leicester began to decay; and the ancient confederacy of the Cinque Ports (Winchelsea alone excepted) was already in decline before the outbreak of the Hundred Years War. Yet the evidence as a whole hardly warrants us in projecting back into the fourteenth century the general decay of the old corporate boroughs which had become evident by the end of the Middle Ages. Apart from normal fluctuations of trade and industry and the incidence of plague, many towns seem to have maintained themselves in a state of reasonable, and a few of mounting, prosperity. York, the second city in the kingdom and a shire incorporate by 1398, with an unrivalled position on a great tidal river, was well established as a great commercial and industrial centre. Bristol, a shire by 1373, had long since outgrown its original city walls and even before the end of Edward III's reign, it was said that all the corn produced within ten leagues did not suffice to feed the population of a great port which was fast becoming also a notable centre of industry. The fortunes of Southampton fluctuated and its very small population of 1,728 indicates a period of slump;

From May McKisak, *The Fourteenth Century* (Oxford, 1959), pp. 380–381. Reprinted by permission of The Clarendon Press.

but the rise of the Cotswold flocks had shifted the main source of the Italian wool supply from east to west and, although the Venetian carracks continued to prefer London, Southampton gradually established itself as the principal centre of Genoese shipping and as a market for the sale of the alum, wood, and fruits absorbed by the towns and villages of the south-western shires. Plymouth, in 1377 the fourth largest borough in England, derived its prosperity from fish, tin, and a general carrying trade. Extensive building projects at Norwich under Richard II, the existence of no fewer than thirty-eight gilds at Beverley in 1390, the recovery of Ipswich in the nineties after a long period of depression, all point to a fair degree of prosperity. Moreover, the century saw the rise of more than one town of hitherto limited importance. Edward I's borough of Kingston-on-Hull by the nineties was sharing with London the greater part of the northern cloth trade. Coventry, already by 1377 the fifth town in the country and nearly as large as Plymouth, had gained independence of its joint overlords, the prior and Queen Isabella, obtained a charter in 1345 and a mayor three years later, and was thus free to take full advantage of its nodal position in the road system and of its own rapidly expanding drapery business to enlist the royal family among its customers and to raise the most splendid perpendicular tower in England. The episcopal cities of Salisbury and Winchester by the middle of the fourteenth century were among the foremost industrial communities in the country.

SUGGESTIONS FOR ADDITIONAL READING

This bibliography, intended to carry the reader beyond the histories and sources excerpted here, moves from the general to the particular. Two books containing essays which present many points of view current in the social sciences are *The Study of Urbanization,* ed. Philip M. Hauser and Leo F. Schnore (New York, 1965), and *Urbanism and Urbanization,* ed. Nels Anderson (Leiden, 1964). The analyses of a great pioneer in sociology have been collected and translated as Max Weber, *The City* (Glencoe, Ill., 1958).

A history of urbanization shorter and simpler than that of Lewis Mumford is Arthur Korn, *History Builds the Town* (London, 1953). For medieval Europe alone there are a thoughtful essay and illustrative documents in John H. Mundy and Peter Riesenberg, *The Medieval Town* (Princeton, 1958), and Carl B. Troedsson has written a useful survey in *The Growth of the Western City during the Middle Ages* (Göteborg, 1959). A full bibliography and a chapter on "The Rise of the Towns" by Hans van Werveke are provided in the *Cambridge Economic History of Europe,* Vol. III (Cambridge, Eng., 1963). The most thorough study of the early history of European towns since that of Henri Pirenne is Edith Ennen, *Frühgeschichte der europäischen Stadt* (Bonn, 1953). Valuable materials from Jewish sources (and some questionable conclusions) are given by Irving A. Agus, *Urban Civilization in Pre-Crusade Europe* (New York, 1965). A special aspect of urban origins is treated in "Medieval Town Planning," in *The Collected Papers of Thomas Frederick Tout,* Vol. III (Manchester, 1934), 59–92.

For national and regional studies one should turn first to Erwin A. Gutkind's multivolume *International History of City Development* (Glencoe, Ill., 1964–). This monumental work may be supplemented by Gerald L. Burke, *The Making of Dutch Towns* (London, 1956) and Mikail N. Tikhomirov, *The Towns of Ancient Rus* (Moscow, 1959). *Les origines des villes polonais,* ed. Pierre Francastel (Paris, 1960), summarizes recent Polish scholarship in a Western European language. Two non-English sections of Great Britain are treated in Edward Arthur Lewis, *The Mediaeval Boroughs of Snowdonia* (London, 1912), and William Mackay Mackenzie, *The Scottish Burghs* (Edinburgh, 1949).

For the history of English towns a good place to begin is James Tait's lecture to the British Academy in 1922, "The Study of Early Municipal History in England," published in a slightly revised form in his *Medieval English Borough* (Manchester, 1936). The contributions of that book and their relation to the theories of Carl Stephenson are discussed by Reginald R. Darlington, "The Early History of English Towns," *History,* N.S. XXIII (1938), pp. 141–150. There is an excellent chapter on "Towns and Trade" by Eleanora M. Carus-Wilson in *Medieval England,* new ed. by Austin Lane Poole (Oxford, 1958), a compilation which contains fine chapters on many other topics, including coinage and castles. A special type of medieval town is analysed by Norman M. Trenholme, *The English Monastic Boroughs,* The University of Missouri Studies, Vol. II, No. 3 (Columbia, Mo., 1927).

As an introduction to the general history of early medieval England, Henry R. Loyn, *Anglo-Saxon England and the Norman Conquest* (London, 1962), is an excellent book whose treatment of economic history compliments the standard work in the Oxford History of England, Frank M. Stenton, *Anglo-Saxon England,* 2nd ed. (Oxford, 1947).

There are perceptive comments on the use and misuse of evidence from the early middle ages in Frederick T. Wainwright, *Archaeology and Place-Names and His-*

tory (London, 1962). Percy H. Reaney's *The Origin of English Place-Names* (London, 1960) is a fuller introduction to that particular subject. For current work in English archaeology consult the journal *Mediaeval Archaeology* (London, 1957–). On coinage see Henry R. Loyn, "Boroughs and Mints," in *Anglo-Saxon Coins,* ed. Reginald H. Dolley (London, 1961). R. Weldon Finn, *An Introduction to Domesday Book* (London, 1963), is a simple guide to complicated material. There are good pictures of towns in Maurice W. Beresford and J. K. S. St. Joseph, *Medieval England, an Aerial Survey* (Cambridge, Eng., 1958), and Geoffrey H. Martin, *The Town* (London, 1961).

Charles Gross' influential book *The Gild Merchant* (Oxford, 1890) is criticized by D. J. V. Fisher, "Economic Institutions in the Towns of Medieval England," in *Recueils de la Société Jean Bodin, VII, La Ville, Deuxième partie: Institutions économiques et sociales* (Brussels, 1955), a collection whose multilingual contributions advance comparative history. Emile Coornaert's important revisionist article, "Les ghildes médiévales," in *Revue historique,* CXCIX (1948), pp. 22–55, 208–243, is strangely ignored by many English historians.

The ever-growing set of the *Victoria History of the Counties of England* (Westminster, 1900–) is a mine of information for local history. Besides such materials as translations of Domesday Book and diagrams of ancient earthworks and castles, it contains monographic studies of a number of boroughs, including Leicester, York, Wilton and Salisbury.

Since there are many towns in England and even more town histories, a large class can collaborate by parcelling out individual towns for study. A few of the best books are Frederic William Maitland, *Township and Borough* (Cambridge, Eng., 1898), an old but characteristically lucid work on Cambridge; James Tait, *Medieval Manchester and the Beginnings of Lancashire* (Manchester, 1904); Mary D. Lobel, *The Borough of Bury St. Edmunds* (Oxford, 1935); J. W. Francis Hill, *Medieval Lincoln* (Cambridge, Eng., 1948); Ruth Fasnacht, *History of the City of Oxford* (Oxford, 1954); Gwyn Williams, *Medieval London, from Commune to Capital* (London, 1963); Alan Rogers, ed., *The Making of Stamford* (Leicester, 1965); and William G. Urry, *Canterbury Under the Angevin Kings* (London, 1967), accompanied by large-scale, highly detailed maps showing individual properties.

Among the good shorter studies are two articles by Herbert P. R. Finberg, "The Borough of Tavistock," in W. G. Hoskins and H. P. R. Finberg, *Devonshire Studies* (London, 1952), and "The Genesis of the Gloucestershire Towns," in his *Gloucestershire Studies* (Leicester, 1957). See also Levi Fox, "The Early History of Coventry," *History,* N.S., XXX (1945), 21–37, and E. M. Carus-Wilson, "The First Half Century of the Borough of Stratford-on-Avon," *Economic History Review,* 2nd. ser., XVIII (1965), 46–63.

The most useful sources of compressed information on the early history of particular towns are old works, Samuel Lewis, *A Topographical Dictionary of England,* 5 vols. (London, 7th ed., 1849), and the *Encyclopaedia Britannica,* whose articles on English towns have been only slightly revised since the 11th ed. (1910). The standard bibliography is Charles Gross, *A Bibliography of British Municipal History* (Cambridge, Mass., 1897), reprinted photographically (Leicester, 1966) with an introductory essay by Geoffrey H. Martin, who is preparing a continuation. Also highly useful is Wilfrid Bonser, *Anglo-Saxon and Celtic Bibliography (450–1087),* 2 vols. (Oxford and Berkeley, 1957). Peter Stockham and others, *British Local History; a Selected Bibliography* (London, 1964) is a handy list. Current work is announced in the *Urban History Newsletter* (Dept. of Economic History, University of Leicester, 1963–).

2 3 4 5 6 7 8 9 0